REVISED ORDINANCES

OF THE

CITY OF GALESBURG,

WITH THE

CITY CHARTER AND AMENDMENTS,

AND THE

GRADED SCHOOL CHARTER,

WITH SUNDRY SPECIAL LAWS OF THE STATE OF ILLINOIS, RELATING TO THE GOVERNMENT OF TOWNS AND CITIES, WITH A SHORT STATEMENT

OF THE

SETTLEMENT OF GALESBURG,

ITS

POPULATION, GOVERNMENT, &c.

REVISED BY

W. A. WOOD, City Clerk,

AND

PUBLISHED BY ORDER OF THE CITY COUNCIL.

GALESBURG, ILL.:
J. H. SHERMAN, BOOK AND JOB PRINTER.
1863.

TO THE PUBLIC.

The only apology I have to offer for the publication of this Book, is the following order passed by the City Council, October 5th, 1863:

"Voted, That the City Clerk be, and is hereby authorized to prepare and procure the publication of two hundred volumes of the Revised Ordinances of this city."

W. A. WOOD,
City Clerk.

HISTORICAL SKETCH.

The City of Galesburg, Knox County, Illinois, is situated on the Chicago, Burlington and Quincy Rail Road, 168 miles south-west from Chicago, and 100 miles north-east from Quincy.

The Peoria and Oquawka Rail Road crosses the track of the C. B. & Q. at this point, being 42 miles east of Burlington, Iowa, and 47 miles west from Peoria.

In 1836, late in the Autumn, about thirty families from Western New York removed to what is now the town of Galesburg, and spent their first winter in the edge of Henderson Grove, and in the Spring of 1837, began to build what is now called the City of Galesburg.

In 1845, the population had reached about 300; since that time, until the present, the growth has been gradual and steady; and in October, 1863, the population of the City was 6,475, exclusive of students in the colleges here from abroad, which will make the number of inhabitants now about 7,000.

There are two Colleges—Knox College and Lombard University, besides a very excellent and highly flourishing Seminary for young ladies,—under the care of the Trustees of Knox College—now in successful operation in this City.

There are twelve Churches, and a system of Graded Free Schools has been inaugurated, in which an average attendance of 1,000 children are taught.

The City Government was first inaugurated in April, 1857, when the following City Officers were chosen, namely:

CITY OFFICERS.

1857.

Mayor—HENRY R. SANDERSON.

Aldermen,

J. H. Sherman, Edwin Post,
James F. Dunn, J. W. Cothren,
Marcus Belden, E. M. Jordan.

City Clerk—O. S. Pitcher.
" Marshal—Frederick P. Sisson.
" Assessor—David Sanborn.
" Treasurer—A. M. Phelps.
" Street Commissioner—John Burlingham.

1858.

Mayor—SAMUEL W. BROWN.

Aldermen,

Elisha C. Field, Edwin Post,
Jacob D. Hand, J. W. Cothren,
E. R. Adams, E. M. Jordan.

City Clerk—William A. Wood.
" Marshal—Timothy Walker.
" Assessor—David Sanborn.
" Treasurer—George Davis.
" Street Commissioner—Lyman Arnold.

1859.

Mayor—JOHN C. STEWART.

Aldermen,

Elisha C. Field, George I. Bergen,
Jacob D. Hand, Reuben Heflin,
E. R. Adams, Clark E. Carr.

City Clerk—William A. Wood.
" Marshal—Henry Moore.
" Assessor—David Sanborn.
" Treasurer—George Davis.
" Street Commissioner—Lyman Arnold.

1860.

MAYOR—JAMES F. DUNN.

Aldermen,

WALTER BRINKERHOFF, GEORGE I. BERGEN,
HENRY S. HURD, REUBEN HEFLIN,
LOYAL C. FIELD, CLARK E. CARR.

City Clerk—WILLIAM A. WOOD.
" Marshal—HENRY MOORE.
" Assessor—JOHN F. EDGERTON.
" Treasurer—BENJAMIN F. HOLCOMB.
" Street Commissioner—PETER L. HAWKINSON.

1861.

MAYOR—ALFRED KNOWLES.

Aldermen,

J. R. GORDON, WM. PENN FRAILEY,
HENRY S. HURD, S. S. CHEENEY,
LOYAL C. FIELD, JOB SWIFT.

City Clerk—WILLIAM A. WOOD.
" Marshal—HENRY MOORE.
" Assessor—JOHN F. EDGERTON.
" Treasurer—BENJAMIN F. HOLCOMB.
" Street Commissioner—PETER L. HAWKINSON.

1862.

MAYOR—ALBERT REED.

Aldermen,

JOSIAS GRANT, WM. PENN FRAILEY,
HENRY S. HURD, S. S. CHEENEY,
TIMOTHY NASH, JOB SWIFT.

City Clerk—WILLIAM A. WOOD,
" Marshal—GEORGE EKINS.
" Assessor—DAVID SANBORN.
" Treasurer—ISAAC DELANO.
" Street Commissioner—PETER L. HAWKINSON.

1863.

MAYOR—JAMES F. DUNN.

Aldermen,

TIMOTHY MOSHIER, PETER SCHOBERG,
HENRY S. HURD, LAUREN C. CONGER,
TIMOTHY NASH, WARREN S. BELLOWS.

City Clerk—WILLIAM A. WOOD.
" Marshal—GEORGE EKINS.
" Assessor—JOHN F. EDGERTON.
" Treasurer—ISAAC DELANO.
" Street Commissioner—PATRICK CHAPLAN.

1864.

MAYOR—JOHN A. MARSHALL.

Aldermen,

ELISHA C. FIELD, SOCRATES S. CHENEY,
FREDERICK P. SISSON, JAMES LARKIN,
WARREN C. WILLARD, WARREN S. BELLOWS.

City Clerk—WILLIAM A. WOOD.
" Marshall—HORACE H. WILLSIE.
" Assessor—GEORGE EKINS.
" Treasurer—ISAAC DELANO.
" Street Commissioner—PATRICK CHAPLAN.

STATE LAWS.

WEIGHTS AND MEASURES.

An Act to amend an act concerning weights and measures.

Be it enacted by the people of the State of Illinois, represented in the General Assembly:

SEC. 1. That whenever any of the following articles shall be contracted for, or sold, or delivered, and no special contract or agreement shall be made to the contrary, the weight per bushel shall be as follows, to-wit: Shelled corn, fifty-six (56) pounds; corn in the ear, seventy (70) pounds; wheat, sixty (60) pounds; rye, fifty-six (56) pounds; oats, thirty two (32) pounds; barley, forty-eight (48) pounds; Irish potatoes, sixty (60) pounds; sweet potatoes, fifty-five (55) pounds; white beans, sixty (60) pounds; castor beans, forty-six (46) pounds; clover seed, sixty (60) pounds; timothy seed, forty-five (45) pounds; flax seed, fifty-six (56) pounds; hemp seed, forty-four (44) pounds; blue-grass seed, fourteen (14) pounds; buckwheat, fifty-two (52) pounds; dried peaches, thirty-three (33) pounds; dried apples, twenty-four (24) pounds; onions, fifty-seven (57) pounds; salt, fifty (50) pounds; stone coal, eighty (80) pounds; malt, thirty-eight (38) pounds; bran, twenty (20) pounds; turnips, fifty-five (55) pounds; hair, [plastering], eight (8) pounds; unslaked lime, eighty (80) pounds; corn meal, forty-eight (48) pounds; fine salt, fifty-five (55) pounds.

SEC. 2. All laws and parts of laws inconsistent with this act are hereby repealed.

Approved February 14 1855.

TOWNS AND CITIES.

An Act to incorporate towns and cities.

Be it enacted by the people of the State of Illinois, represented in the General Assembly:

Sec. 1. That any incorporated town or city in this state may have power to provide by ordinance that every person against whom any judgment may hereafter be recovered in favor of said town or city for a penalty or fine for a breach of any ordinance, instead of being committed to jail may be required to labor on the streets until the whole fine and costs shall be paid, at the same rate per day as may be allowed as a forfeiture for a failure to perform street labor under the direction of the street commissioner.

Sec. 2. The corporate authorities of any city or town in this state may have power to declare what shall be a nuisance, and to prevent and remove the same as much as one-half mile beyond the limits of the corporation, with full power to impose a fine for a violation of any ordinance to that effect.

Sec. 3. Whenever it may become necessary to pave or grade any streets or front lots, or to fill up or alter any lot that may be declared to be a nuisance, said corporate authorities may have power, upon the failure of the owner of any lot to pave, grade, or fill up said lot, or to pay the taxes or fine that may be assessed on the owner or owners thereof, to require that said lot, or so much thereof as may be necessary, shall be sold for the payment of the tax or fine and costs in the manner authorized for the collection of other taxes, and all assessments so made shall constitute a lien on said lot.

Sec. 4. The corporate authorities of all towns and cities incorporated under chapter twenty-five, entitled "corporations," of the revised code, or under any special act, shall have power to pass all the ordinances and by-laws, and possess all the powers authorized under the laws and amendatory acts incorporating either of the cities of Springfield or Quincy; Provided, that towns containing a population of less than fifteen hundred white inhabitants shall have no other officers or allow any other compensation than is allowed under chapter twenty-five of the revised code, unless expressly authorized by law.

* * * * * * * * *

Sec. 8. The inhabitants of any town or city in the corporate name may purchase, receive and hold real estate beyond the limits as [of] the corporate limits for the purpose of burying-grounds.

Sec. 9. Whenever the corporate authorities of any town or city may wish to have the taxes, authorized to be levied under and by virtue of their respective charters, or under the general act, upon filing a certificate of the rate authorized under the authority of the said corporation in the office of the clerk of the county court, it shall be the duty of the collector of taxes for the state and county to collect the taxes for said town or city upon the assessment of the value of all the property within the limits of said corporation, as ascertained by the assessment for state and county purposes, and enforce the payment thereof in the same manner and with all the rights, power and authority as he has to collect state and county taxes, and shall pay the same over to the order of the corporate authorities at the same time he is required to pay over the county revenue, and the court of the proper county shall render judgment and order sale of any lot or tract for the non-payment of the tax and cost due said town or city, as is or may be provided for state and county taxes; and judgment and sale shall be rendered for the aggregate amount due for county, state and town, or city taxes. The collector shall receive the same compensation for collecting the taxes for any town or city as is allowed for the collection of state and county revenue, to be paid out of the funds of the corporation, and he shall be liable on his bond for the faithful performance of the duties required under this act.

Sec. 10. This act to take effect from and after its passage.

Approved February 10, 1849.

GOVERNMENT OF TOWNS AND CITIES—POLICE MAGISTRATES.

An Act for the better government of towns and cities, and to amend the charters thereof.

Be it enacted by the people of the State of Illinois, represented in the General Assembly:

Sec. 1. That there shall be established in each of the cities of this state inferior courts of civil and criminal jurisdiction, which shall [be] called police-magistrates courts.

SEC. 2. That there shall be elected in each of the incorporated towns and cities of this state, the population of which shall not exceed six thousand, an officer who shall be styled police magistrate of the city of , or town of , as the case may be; in each city of this state having a population of over six thousand and not exceeding twelve thousand there shall be elected two police magistrates; and in the cities of this state whose population shall exceed twelve thousand there shall be elected three police magistrates. Said magistrates shall be elected by the legal voters of such city or town at the next regular election for city or town officers, and every four years thereafter.

SEC. 3. Said police magistrates, when elected, shall be commissioned and qualified in the same manner as justices of the peace are, and shall have, in their respective counties, the same jurisdiction, powers and emoluments as other justices of the peace in this state; and they shall also have jurisdiction in all cases arising under the ordinances of their respective towns and cities, and for any breaches thereof where the amount claimed shall not exceed one hundred dollars; and in all cases arising under the ordinances of towns and cities said magistrates shall be entitled to the same fees as justices of the peace now are for similar services, and to be collected in the same manner: Provided, the city or town authorities of any such town or city may make such additional allowance to such police magistrates as they may deem just and expedient; and in all cases arising under the ordinances of any such town or city, change of venue shall be allowed from one police magistrate to another in cities where there is more than one such magistrate; and in all other towns and cities, from such police magistrate to the nearest justice of the peace, to be applied for in the same manner and granted on the same conditions and in the same manner as changes of venue from justices of the peace now are.

SEC. 4. The rules of practice and proceeding before such police magistrate shall conform to the practice and proceedings before justices of the peace, except in cases where such rules of practice and proceedings shall be changed or modified by the charter of such town or city; in which case such rules of practice and proceedings shall conform to the said charters.

SEC. 5. The city marshals of such towns or cities, and all constables of the county in which said town or city may be situated, and all the town or police constables of such towns or cities respectively, shall be and are hereby authorized to execute all process and orders issued or made by said police magistrates in their respective counties.

SEC. 6. Appeals shall be allowed from the decision of police magistrates in all cases, to be applied for and taken in the same manner that appeals from justices of the peace may be taken.

SEC. 7. This act to take effect and be in force from and after its passage.

Approved February 27, 1854.

AN ACT to amend an act entitled "An act for the better government of towns and cities, and to amend the charters thereof," approved Feb. 27, 1854.

Be it enacted by the people of the State of Illinois, represented in the General Assembly:

SEC. 1. That all police magistrates, when elected, shall severally hold their offices for the term of four years, and until others are elected and qualified; and in case of the death, resignation or removal from the town or city of any of the said police magistrates, their offices shall be deemed thereby vacated, and such vacancies shall be filled by special elections for that purpose, notified and conducted in the same manner as is now provided by law for special elections for justices of the peace.

SEC. 2. This act shall take effect and be in force from and after its passage.

Approved Feb. 15, 1855.

VACATING TOWN PLATS.

AN ACT to provide for vacating Town Plats.

Be it enacted by the people of the State of Illinois, represented in the General Assembly:

SEC. 1. That in all cases where persons have heretofore or may hereafter lay out towns or sub-divisions of town lots, and the plats and maps thereof shall have been recorded, they, their heirs, assigns or grantees, may, at any time before making sale of any single lot or lots, by executing a writing and causing the same to be recorded in the office in which the plat or map was recorded, declare such map or plat to be vacated; and the execution and recording of such writing shall operate to destroy the force and effect of the recording of the plat or map so vacated, and to divest all public rights in the streets, alleys, commons and public grounds laid down or described in such plat or map; and in cases where any single lot or lots have been sold, the plat or map may be vacated as herein provided by all the owners of lots joining in the execution of the writing aforesaid: *provided*, that no such writing shall be recorded until the execution thereof shall have been acknowledged or proved as is or may be required in respect to deeds.

SEC. 2. The provisions of this act shall not apply to the original map or plat of any town located or laid out as or for a county seat, so long as the county seat shall remain at such town; but plats or maps of additions to such towns or subdivisions of lots included in the recorded plats or maps thereof, may be vacated as herein provided for: *provided, however*, that nothing contained in this act shall authorize the closing or obstructing the public road laid out according to law.

SEC. 3. Any part of a plat or map of a town, addition or sub-division may be vacated under the provisions and subject to the conditions herein contained.

Approved February 16, 1847.

EVIDENCE.

Certified Copies of Corporation Proceedings.

Extract from chapter XL, entitled "Evidence and Depositions."—Revised Statutes.

SEC. 9. Copies of all papers, books or proceedings or parts thereof, appertaining to transactions in their corporate capacity of any town or city heretofore incorporated, or now incorporated, or that may hereafter be incorporated under a general or special law of this state, certified to be true copies by the clerk or keeper of the same, under the seal of said town or city, or under the private seal of said clerk or keeper if there be no public seal, the said clerk or keeper also certifying that he is intrusted with the safe keeping of the originals of which he gives certified copies, shall be received as *prima facie* evidence of the facts so certified in all the courts of this state in any suit or proceeding pending before them.

WARRANTS OF CITIES AND TOWNS.

Chapter CVII.—Revised Statutes, 1845.

SEC. 1. In all cases in which any city or town in this state shall be indebted to any person or persons on any account whatsoever, a warrant or voucher shall be drawn on the treasurer of such city or town for the whole amount due to such person by the tribunal having power to audit and allow claims against such city or town; and such tribunal shall not, in any case, draw more than one warrant or voucher for the amount allowed to one individual at one time.

SEC. 2. No warrant or voucher drawn on the treasurer of any city or town shall be drawn in favor of any other person than the one to whom the same may be due, and such warrant or voucher may be in the form now prescribed by law.

SEC. 3. No treasurer of any city or town in this state shall pay any warrant or voucher drawn on him unless such warrant be presented by the person in whose favor such warrant is drawn, or his assignee, executor or administrator.

SEC. 4. Any officer or officers of any town or city that shall be guilty of violating the provisions of this chapter shall be deemed guilty of a misdemeanor in office, and for every such violation shall be fined in a sum not exceeding five hundred dollars to be recovered by indictment.

Approved March 3, 1845.

CHANGING AND VACATING STREETS.

AN ACT authorizing incorporated cities to change, alter and vacate streets or parts of streets.

Be it enacted by the people of the State of Illinois, represented in the General Assembly:

SEC. 1. That when the corporate authorities of any city may deem it for the best interest of their respective cities that any street or part of a street shall be changed, altered or vacated, said authorities shall have the power, upon petition of the property holders owning property on such street or part of street to change, alter or vacate the same, and to convey by quit-claim deed, all interest which said city may have had in the street or part of a street so vacated, to the owner or owners of lots and lands next to and adjoining the same, upon the payment by such owner or owners of all assessments which may be made against their lots and lands for and on account of benefits to the same arising from such change, alteration or vacation of any street or part of street as aforesaid.

Sec. 2. The benefits and damages caused by changing, altering or vacating any street or part of street as aforesaid shall be assessed and determined in the manner pointed out by the act incorporating such city, or by the ordinances thereof in other cases.

Approved February 15, 1857.

JUDGMENT ON TAX LIST.

An Act to amend the charters of the several towns and cities in this state.

Be it enacted by the people of the State of Illinois, represented in the General Assembly:

Sec. 1. That in all cases when taxes assessed on real estate by the corporate authorities of any city or town in this state, except in the city of Chicago, are not paid within the time fixed by the corporate authorities of any such city or town, it shall be lawful for the collector of any such city or town, after giving notice of such application by advertisement, at least thirty days previously to such application, in some newspaper published in said town or city, or if no newspaper should be published in said town or city, then by posting up printed or written notices of such intended application in at least four of the most public places in such town or city, to apply to the county court of the county in which such delinquent real estate may be situated, and cause judgment to be entered against such delinquent real estate for the amount of taxes due and unpaid and costs. And the said county court shall proceed to hear and determine said application and render judgment against said delinquent real estate in the same manner, and said judgment shall have the like effect as though the said delinquent list had been returned to the county court by the sheriff or collector of the county in the collection of the state or county taxes. And the county court shall issue its precept or order to the collector of said city or town, directing him to sell said real estate at public auction to pay said delinquent taxes and costs, *provided*, that the corporate authorities of such towns or cities shall have full power sary to carry this section into full effect; *and provided, further*, that the corporate authorities of any town or city shall have power to fix the time of such application to the county court and the time of sale of said real estate.

SEC. 2. In all cases where assessments have before been made, or where assessments may hereafter be made, by the corporate authorities of any town or city in this state, on any lot or real estate in such town or city, for the purpose of improving any street, sidewalk or alley in front of such lot or real estate, or for any purpose whatever, either by ordinance, resolution or other proceeding, and such assessment is not paid within the time fixed by the order, resolution or ordinance making such assessment, the corporate authorities of the sev-
to adopt any regulation or proceeding they may deem neces-
eral towns and cities in the state may apply to the county court of the proper county for judgment against said lot or real estate for the amount of said assessment and costs; and the county court, on such application being made, shall render judgment against such lot or real estate for the amount of said assessments and costs, and shall issue its precept to the sheriff of the proper county, commanding him to sell said lot or real estate or so much thereof as may be necessary to pay said judgment and costs, in the same manner and with like effect as if sold upon execution at law; and the corporate authorities of the several towns or cities shall have full power to provide by resolution or ordinance for the making or levying any such assessment, and they shall have power to fix the time of payment, and the kind and time of notice of such assessment, and of the said application to the county court, and the corporate authorities of any town or city shall have full and complete authority to adopt any rule, regulation or proceeding which they may deem necessary to carry the provisions of this section into full and complete effect.

SEC. 3. This act to take effect from and after its passage.

Approved March 1, 1854.

QUALIFICATION OF VOTERS, AND TO PREVENT ILLEGAL VOTING.

An Act to provide for ascertaining the qualifications of voters and to prevent illegal voting.

Whereas, The right of suffrage is the highest privilege of the citizen, and should be guarded with proper vigilance against intrusion and fraud; for the purpose, therefore, of ascertaining the persons who may be entitled to vote at the several elections held under the laws of this State, and to prevent illegal voting thereat,

Be it enacted by the people of the State of Illinois represented in the General Assembly:

§ 1. That to constitute residence under the Constitution and election laws of the State, a permanent abode is necessary, and at all elections, general or special, held in any town, city, district or ward, every person offering to vote who is not personally known to the Judges and Inspectors of Election to have such permanent abode and to have resided in such election district for the space of sixty days immediately preceding such election, shall, if his vote be challenged, take the 'oath required by law, and in addition thereto, swear or affirm to his place of residence, specifying the particular place and house in which he resides, and stating how long he has there resided, and his business or employment; and if he has not resided in such house for sixty days immediately preceding such election, he shall state where and in what houses he has resided for the last sixty days, and in addition thereto such voter so challenged shall be required to produce two witnesses, both of whom are personally known to said judges of said election, and residents in the precinct, district or ward, or shall be proved by some legal voter or voters of the precinct or district in which said vote is offered to be voted therein, who shall be known to such judges, and each of them shall take the following oath, to be administered by one of the judges of said election:

"I do solemnly swear or affirm (as the case may be) that "I am a resident of this election district, and entitled to vote "at this election, and that I have been a resident of this elec- "tion district for one year last past, and that I am well ac-

"quainted with the voter whose vote is now offered, that he "is an actual and *bona fide* resident of this election district, "and that he has resided in this State for one year last past."

§ 2. If any judge of any district shall permit any voter to vote whose vote is so challenged, without the proof required in the first section of this act, or shall knowingly and wilfully permit any person to testify as a witness contrary to the provisions of this act, he shall be deemed guilty of a high misdemeanor, and on conviction thereof, shall be fined in the sum of one thousand dollars, and imprisoned in the county jail for six months.

§ 3. If any witness or voter whose vote is so challenged and sworn under the provision of the first section of this act, shall knowingly, wilfully and corruptly swear falsely, he shall be deemed guilty of perjury, and upon conviction thereof, imprisoned in the Penitentiary for any term not less than three nor more than twenty-one years.

§ 4. If any person shall vote more than once at any election held under the authority of the laws of this State, or shall vote at any such election, who is not a qualified voter at the place where he so votes, or shall offer to vote after having once voted at such election, he shall, on conviction thereof, be confined in the Penitentiary for any time not less than one or more than five years.

§ 5. At all elections, general or special, in this State, where the vote is by ballot, if the judges of election are satisfied, under the provisions of this act and the other laws of this State relating to elections, that the person offering the vote is the legal voter, he shall endorse the back of the ticket offered, the number corresponding with the vote on the poll book, and put such ticket immediately in the ballot box, and the clerk of the election shall enter the name of the voter and his number in the poll book.

§ 6. At the close of the polls the poll boks shall be signed by the judges; and attested by the clerks. The names therein contained shall then be counted, and the number set down at the foot of the poll books.

§ 7. All the ballots counted by the judges of election, shall, after being read, be strung on a strong thread or twine, in the order in which they have been read, and shall then be carefully enveloped and sealed up by the judges, who shall direct the same to the officer or officers to whom by law they are required to return the poll books, and shall be delivered, together with said poll books, to said officer or officers, who shall carefully preserve said poll books for six months, and at the expiration of that time shall destroy them, and in all cases of contested election, the parties contesting the same shall have the right to have the said package of ballots opened,, and said ballots referred to by witnesses for the purpose of such contest: but said ballots shall only be so examined and referred to in the presence of the officer having the custody thereof.

§ 8. The provisions of this act shall apply to all general and special elections hereafter held in the State, whether for general, town, municipal or other offices, and no person shall be considered as having resided in any ward, or election district, or precinct, unless he shall have had a permanent abode therein for at least thirty days immediately preceding such election.

§ 9. No liquor or other intoxicating drinks shall be sold or given away at retail, nor shall any bar-room or place where liquor or intoxicating drinks are sold at retail, be open upon such election day, and it shall be the duty of the sheriff, constables, public officers and magistrates to see that the provisions of this section are enforced, and any violation of its provisions shall be prosecuted and punished in the same manner and to the same extent as the keeping of tippling houses open on Sunday; or the first day of the week, is now punished by law.

§ 10. This act shall take effect and be in force from and after its passage.

Shelby M. Cullom,
Speaker of the House of Representatives.

Francis A. Hoffman,
Speaker of the Senate.

Approved Feb. 22, 1861. Richard Yates, Governor.

RULES OF ORDER AND BUSINESS

OF THE

CITY COUNCIL.

RULE I. The regular meetings of the City Council shall be held on every Monday evening, only as otherwise ordered.

RULE II. The Council can adjourn to any intermediate time between the regular meetings.

RULE III. When any exigency may arise, the Mayor or any two aldermen, may call a special meeting of the Council, by giving at least six hours' notice to each alderman, then in the city, of the time and place of meeting.

RULE IV. The Council shall be called to order, at precisely the hour to which it stood adjourned, the roll of members called, and absentees noted.

RULE V. The Mayor shall preside at all meetings when present; in his absence the acting Mayor who shall be elected by ballot, shall preside.

RULE VI. A majority of the aldermen shall constitute a quorum for the transaction of business, and shall have power to send the city marshal for absent members who are in the city.

RULE VII. A refusal to attend when so summoned, unless a valid excuse is shown, shall be considered a contempt of the Council, and punished according to their discretion.

RULE VIII. The Mayor shall give the casting vote in case of a tie, shall enforce the rules and preserve order, shall appoint all committees unless otherwise ordered by the Council, and may speak to any question under consideration, by calling to the chair some member to preside in his place.

Rule IX. The acting Mayor shall have the same powers and discharge the same duties as the Mayor, in the absence of the latter.

Rule X. No personal charges, insinuations or inuendoes shall be made against any member in debate or during a session of the Council, and in case they are made the offending party shall be required to take his seat, and be punished for contempt, as the Council may determine.

Rule XI. Any two members may demand a vote by yeas and nays, upon any motion pending before the Council.

Rule XII. No motion to reconsider shall be entertained after the meeting, in which the business sought to be reconsidered was transacted.

Rule XIII. All ordinances and resolutions in the nature of ordinances, shall be read twice before their final adoption, once of which may be by their title.

Rule XIV. The following shall be the standing committees of the Council, each composed of two members:

1. Claims and Einance.
2. Streets and Improvements.
3. Miscellaneous business.

Rule XV. The standing committees shall be considered the organ of the Council for investigations and report, but shall not be authorized to take definite action without the order of the Council.

Rule XVI. All reports of committees, and all resolutions shall be submitted in writing.

Rule XVII. The following order of business shall be observed:

1. Calling the roll of members.
2. Reading the minutes of last meeting.
3. Presentation of petitions.
4. Resolutions.
5. Reports of committees.
6. Unfinished business.
7. New business.

Rule XVIII. No rule shall be suspended, except by a two-thirds vote of the Council.

Rule XIX. Before the commencement of each session the clerk shall furnish the presiding officer a regular callender of business to come under consideration of the Council during that meeting.

Rule XX. These rules may be altered or amended by a majority vote, one week's previous notice of the intended amendment having been given.

CITY CHARTER.

AN ACT TO INCORPORATE THE CITY OF GALESBURG.

ARTICLE I.

BOUNDARIES, GENERAL POWERS AND WARDS.

SEC. 1. Territory erected into the city of Galesburg.
2. General powers of the Corporation.
3. Wards, boundaries of, power to create additional wards.

SECTION 1. *Be it enacted by the people of the State of Illinois, represented in the General Assembly,* That all the district of country in the county of Knox, and State of Illinois, consisting of the tracts of land known as the west half of the southwest quarter of section one, the south half of section two, the south half of section three, the southeast quarter and east half of the southwest quarter of section four, and the east half of the northwest quarter and the east half of the southwest quarter of section nine, the east half of section nine, sections ten and eleven, the west half of the northwest quarter and the west half of the southwest quarter of section twelve, the west half of the northwest quarter and the west [half] of the southwest quarter of section thirteen, sections fourteen and fifteen, the east half of section sixteen, the east half of the northwest quarter and the east half of the southwest quarter of section sixteen, the east half of the northwest quarter of section twenty-one, the northwest quarter of section twenty-one, the north half of section twenty-two, the north half of [section] twenty-three, and the west half of the northwest quarter of section twenty-four, in township eleven (11) north, one (1) east, is hereby erected into a city, by the name of "The City of Galesburg."

§ 2. The inhabitants of said city shall be a corporation, by the name of "The City of Galesburg," and by that name shall have perpetual succession, sue and be sued, and complain and defend in any court; may make and use a common seal, and altar and change it at pleasure; may take, hold and purchase such real, personal or mixed estate as the purposes of the corporation may require, within or without the limits of the city, and may sell, lease or dispose of the same for the benefit of the city.

§ 3. The city of Galesburg shall divide into six wards, the boundaries of which shall be as follows:

The territory bounded on the north by the center line of Main street, on the south by the center line of South street, on the east by the center line of Seminary street, on the west by the center line of West street, shall be called the first ward.

The territory bounded on the north by the center line of North street, on the south by the first ward, on the east by the center line of Seminary street, on the west by the center line of West street, shall be called the second ward.

The territory bounded on the west by the center line of West street and by the same line extended to the northern limits of the city, on the south by the center line of North street and the same extended to the eastern limits of the city, and bounded on the north and east by the city limits, shall be called the third ward.

The territory bounded on the north by the third ward, on the west by the center line of Seminary street and the same being extended to the southern limits of the city, and on the east and south by the city limits, shall be called the fourth ward.

The territory bounded on the east by the fourth ward, on the north by the center line of South street and the same line extended to the western limits of the city, and on the south and west by the city limits, shall be called the fifth ward.

The territory bounded on the south by the fifth ward, on the east by the first, second and third wards, on the north and west by the city limits, shall be called the sixth ward.

The boundaries of the said wards may be, by the city council, changed, from time to time. The city council may create additional wards, as occasion may require, and fix the boundaries thereof.

Article II.

OFFICERS—THEIR ELECTION AND APPOINTMENT.

§ 1. The municipal government of the city shall consist of a city council; to be composed of the mayor, and one alderman from each ward. The other officers of the corporation shall be as follows: A city clerk, a city marshal, a city treasurer, a city attorney, a city assessor, and a street commissioner, a city surveyor and engineer, who, in addition to the duties prescribed by this act, shall perform such other duties as may be prescribed by ordinance. There shall be such other officers, servants and agents as may be provided by ordinance, to be appointed by the city council, and to perform such duties as may be prescribed by the ordinance.

§ 2. All officers, ro be elected or appointed under this act, except alderman and such as are otherwise provided for hereby, shall hold their offices one year and until the election or appointment and qualification of their successors respectively. All other officers mentioned in this act, and not otherwise specially provided for, shall be appointed by the city council, by ballot, on the second Monday of April of each year, or as soon thereafter as may be; but the city council may specially authorize the appointment of watchmen and policemen by the mayor, to continue in office during the pleasure of the city council: *Provided*, the mayor and city marshal may be authorized to remove them from office, for good cause. All officers elected to fill vacancies, except where especially provided for, shall hold for the unexpired term only, and when appointed to fill vacancies, until the next general election, and until the election or appointment and qualification of their successors.

§ 3. The several wards of the city shall be represented in the city council by one alderman from each ward, who shall be a *bona fide* resident thereof. The aldermen shall hold their offices for two years, from and after their election, and until the election and qualification of their successors; but the aldermen elected in the first, third, and fifth wards, at the

4

first election held under this act, shall hold their offices for one year and till their successors are qualified only; but at the annual election in April, 1858, there shall be elected aldermen for the first, third and fifth wards, who shall hold their offices for two years, from the time of their election.

§ 4. If from any cause there shall not be a quorum of aldermen, the clerk shall appoint a time and place for holding a special election to supply such vacancies, and to appoint judges thereof, if necessary. If any alderman shall remove from the ward represented by him his office shall thereby become vacant. If there should be a failure by the people to elect any officer herein required to be elected the city council shall forthwith order a new election.

§ 5. Any officer elected or appointed to any office may be removed from such office, by a vote of two-thirds of all aldermen authorized by law to be elected; but no officer shall be removed, except for good cause, nor unless first furnished with the charges against him, and heard in his defense; and the city council shall have power to compel the attendance of witnesses and the production of papers, when necessary for the purposes of such trial, and shall proceed within ten days, to hear and determine upon the merits of the case; and if such officer shall neglect to appear and answer to such charges, then the city council may declare the office vacant: *Provided*, this section shall not be deemed to apply to any officer appointed by the city council. Such officer may be removed at any time, by a vote of two-thirds, as aforesaid, in their discretion; but any officer may be suspended until the deposition of the charges preferred.

§ 6. Whenever any vacancy shall oocur in the office of mayor or alderman, such vacancy shall be filled by a new election; and the city council shall order such special elections, within ten days after the happening of such vacancy. Any vacancy occuring in any other office may be filled by appointment of the city council, but no special election shall be held to fill vacancies if more than nine months of the time ha s expired.

§ 7. All citizens of the United States, qualified to vote at any election held under this act, shall be qualified to hold any office ereated by this act.

§ 8. When two or more candidates for any elective office shall have an equal number of votes for such office, the election shall be determined by the casting of lots, in the presence of the city council.

Article III.

ELECTIONS.

§ 1. A general election shall be held in each ward of the city, on the first Monday of April next. The time in said day and the place of such elections in each ward shall be determined by the trustees of the town of Galesburg, who shall give six days' notice thereof, posted in one public place in every ward; and they shall also appoint three inspectors of election, for each ward. In case the said trustees should fail to appoint the time and place of such elections and the inspectors thereof, the qualified electors in each ward may assemble at any place in such ward and appoint inspectors from the voters present. At such election shall be chosen a mayor, one alderman in each ward—the alderman to be voted for only by the residents of the ward for which he is elected to represent—a city clerk, a city marshal, a city treasurer, a city assessor, and a city street commissioner; and at the same time and place, the voters of said city shall elect a justice of the peace, as the voters of the district of country included within the corporate limits of the town of Galesburg are authorized to do by the charter of said town, which authority is in no wise changed by this act, only that such justice shall be elected by the voters of the city, instead of the town of Galesburg. Upon each and every first Monday in April thereafter there shall be held a general election for all the the officers required to be elected at such times, by this act or the ordinances of the city.

§ 2. The manner of conducting and voting at the elections held under this act and contesting the same, the keeping of the poll lists, canvassing the votes, and certifying the returns, shall be the same as nearly as may be, as is now or may be hereafter provided by law at general state elections: *provided*, the city council shall have power to regulate elections and appointments of judges thereof. The voting shall be by ballot, and the judges of the election shall take the same oath and shall have the same powers and authority as the judges of general elections. After the closing of the polls the ballots shall be counted in any manner provided by law, and the returns shall be returned, sealed, to the city clerk, within two days after the election; and thereupon the city council shall meet and canvass the same, and declare the result of the election. The persons having the highest number of votes for any office shall be declared elected. It shall be the duty of the city clerk to notify all persons elected or appointed to office, of their elections or appointments; and unless such persons shall qualify within twenty days thereafter, the office shall become vacant. At the first election held on the first Monday of April next, the returns shall be made to the clerk of the board of trustees of the town of Galesburg, and the president and trustees thereof shall meet and canvass the same, and declare the result of the election.

§ 3. No person shall be entitled to vote at any election under this act who is not entitled to vote at state elections, and who has not been a resident of said city at least six months next preceding said election; he shall have been, moreover, an actual resident of the ward in which he proposes to vote for ten days previous to such election, and, if required by any judge or qualified voter, shall take the following oath before he is permitted to vote: "I swear (or affirm) that I am of the age of twenty-one years, that I am a citizen of the United States, (or was a resident of this State at the time of the adoption of the constitution,) and have been a resident of this city six months, and a resident of the state one year, immediately preceding this election, and am now and have been for the last ten days past a resident of this ward, and have not voted at this election." *Provided*, that the voter shall be deemed a resident of the ward in which he is accustomed to lodge.

Article IV.

POWERS AND DUTIES OF OFFICERS.

Sec. 1. Officers shall take oath, to be filed with clerk.
2. Mayor shall see that officers perform their duty.
3. Powers in suppressing riots, and executing laws, &c.
4. To compel execution of books and papers.
5. Salary, how fixed.
6. Shall sign or veto ordinances, hrve power to administer oaths, make acknowledgments, &c.

Sec. 7. Vacancy in office of Mayor, how filled.
8. Members of Council, powers and exemptions.
9. Clerk, term of office, powers and duties.
10. City Assessor. Duties.
11. City Treasurer. Duties.
12. City Marshal. How eligible, duties, powers,

13. City Engineer and Surveyor. Duties, powers.
14. City Assessors. Duties, powers.
15. Street Commissioner. Duties, powers.
16. Officers, power of council over, may require bonds.
17. Officers refusing to deliver papers &c., how dealt with.
18. Officers to be commissioned.

§ 1. Every person chosen or appointed to an executive, judicial or administrative office under this act, shall, before he enters upon the duties of his office, take and subscribe the oath of office prescribed in the constitution of this State, and file the same, duly certified by the officer before whom it was taken, with the city clerk.

§ 2. The Mayor shall preside over the meetings of the city council, and shall take care that the laws of this state and the ordinances of this city are duly enforced, respected and observed within this city; and that all other officers of the city discharge their respective duties; and he shall cause negligence and positive violation of duty to be prosecuted and punished; he shall from time to time give the council such information and recommend such measures as he may deem advantageous to the city.

§ 3. He is hereby authorized to call on any and all white male inhabitants of the city or county, over the age of eighteen years, to aid in the enforcing the laws of the state or the ordinances of the city, and in case of riot to call out the militia to aid in suppressing the same, or carrying into effect any law or ordinance; and any person who shall not obey such call shall forfeit to said city a fine not less than five dollars.

§ 4. He shall have power whenever he may deem it necessary, to require of any of the officers of the city an exhibit of all his books and papers; and he shall have power to execute all acts that may be required of him by this act or any ordinance made in pursuance thereof.

§ 5. He shall receive such salary as may be fixed by ordinance.

§ 6. All ordinances and resolutions shall, before they take effect, be placed in the office of the city clerk, and if the mayor approve thereof he shall sign the same, and such as he shall not approve he shall return to the city council with his objections thereto. Upon the return of any ordinance or resolution by the Mayor, the vote by which the same was passed shall be reconsidered, and if, after such reconsideration, a majority of all the members elected to the city council shall agree, by the "ayes and noes," which shall be entered upon the journal, to pass the same, it shall go into effect; and if the mayor shall neglect to approve or object to any such proceedings for a longer period than three days after the same shall be placed in the clerk's office as aforesaid, the same shall go into effect. He shall, *ex officio*, have power to administer any oath required to be taken by this act or any law of the state, to take depositions, acknowledgements of deeds, mortgages and all other instruments of writing, and certify the same, under the seal of the city, which shall be good and valid in law.

§ 7. In case of vacancy in the office of mayor or of his being unable to perform the duties of his office, by reason of temporary or continued absence or sickness, the city council shall appoint one of its members, by ballot, to preside over their meetings, whose official designation shall be "acting mayor;" and the alderman so appointed shall be vested with all the powers and perform all the duties of mayor until the mayor shall assume his office or the vacancy shall be filled by a new election.

§ 8. The members of the city council shall be, *ex officio*, fire wardens and conservators of the peace, within the city, and shall be exempt from jury duty during their term of office.

§ 9. The clerk shall hold his office for three years; he shall keep the corporate seal and all papers and books belonging to the city; he shall attend all meetings of the city council, and keep a full record of their proceedings on the journals, and copies of all papers duly filed in his office, and transcripts from the journals of the proceedings of the city council certified by him, under the corporate seal, shall be evidence in all courts, in like manner as if the originals were produced; he shall likewise draw all warrants on the treasury and countersign the same, and keep an accurate account thereof, in a book provided for that purpose; he shall, also, keep an accurate account of all receipts and expenditures, in such a manner as the city council shall direct; and he shall have power to administer any oath required to be taken by this act.

§ 10. It shall be the duty of the city attorney to perform all professional services incident to his office, and when required, to furnish written opinions upon questions and subjects submitted to him by the mayor or the city council or its committees.

§ 11. The city treasurer shall collect all taxes and assessments which may be levied by the city council; he shall receive all moneys belonging to the city, and shall keep an accurate account of all receipts and expenditures, in such a manner as the city council shall direct. All moneys shall be drawn from the treasury in pursuance of an order by the city council, by a treasury warrant, signed by the mayor or the presiding officer of the city council, and countersigned by the city clerk. The treasurer shall exhibit to the city council, at least twenty days before the annual election of each year, and oftener, if required, a full and detailed account of all receipts and expenditures since the date of the last annual report, and also the state of the treasury; which shall be filed in the office of the clerk.

§ 12. The city marshal shall hold his office for one year, and he shall not be eligible to said office for more than three years in succession; and shall perform such duties as shall be prescribed by the city council for the preservation of the public peace, the collection of license moneys, fines, or otherwise; he shall possess the powers and authority of a constable at common law, and under the statutes of the state, and receive like fees, but shall not serve civil process, without first entering into bond, as such constable, to be approved by the city council, payable to said city as in other cases; he shall execute and return all process issued by any proper officer under this act or any ordinance in pursuance thereof.

§ 13. The city engineer or surveyor shall have the sole power, under the discretion and control of the city council, to survey within the city limits; and he shall be governed by such rules and ordinances, and receive such fees and emoluments for his services as the council shall direct and prescribe; he shall possess the same powers, in making plats and surveys within the city, as is given by law to county surveyors; and the like effect and validity shall be given to his acts, and to all plats and surveys made by him, as are or may be given by law to the acts, or plats and surveys of the county surveyor; he shall, when required, superintend the construction of all public works ordered by the city, make out the plans and estimates thereof, and contract for the erection of the same; he shall perform all surveying and engineering ordered by the city council; shall, under their direction, establish the grades and boundaries of streets and alleys, but such plans, estimates and contracts, grades and boundaries shall be first reported to the city council and approved by them, or they shall not be valid.

§ 14. The assessor shall perform all duties in relation to the assessing of property, for the purpose of levying the taxes imposed by the city council. In the performance of his duties he shall have the same powers as are or may be given by law to county or town assessors, and be subject to the same liabilities. On completing the assessment lists, and having revised and corrected the same, he shall sign and return them to the city council.

§ 15. The street commissioner shall superintend all local improvements in the city, and carry into effect all orders of the city council in relation thereto. It shall be his duty to superintend and supervise the opening of streets and alleys, and the grading, improving and opening thereof, and the construction and repairing of bridges, culverts and sewers; to order the laying and relaying and repairing of sidewalks; to give notice to the owners of property adjoining such sidewalks, when required, and upon the failure of any person to comply with such notice, to cause the same to be laid or relaid or repaired, and apportion the cost thereof among the persons or lots properly chargeable therewith, and deliver the account thereof to the city clerk, to be laid before the city council; to make plans and estimates of any work ordered in reletion to streets and alleys, culverts or sewers; to keep full and accurate accounts, in appropriate books, of all appropriations made for work pertaining to his office, and of all disbursements thereof, specifying to whom made and on what account, and he shall render monthly accounts thereof to the city council.

§ 16. The city council shall have power, from time t time, to require further and other duties of all officers whose duties are herein prescribed, and prescribe the powers and duties of all officers elected or appointed to any office under this act, whose duties are not herein specified, and fix their compensation. They may, also, require all officers, severally, before they enter upon the duties of their respective offices, to execute a bond to the City of Galesburg, in such sum and with such securities as they may approve, conditioned that they shall faithfully execute the duties of their respective offices, and account for and pay over and deliver all moneys and other property received by them; which bond, with the approval of the city council certified thereon benefit of any person aggrieved by the official act of the officer.

§ 17. If any person, having been an officer of said city, shall not, within ten days after notification and request, deliver to his successor in office all property, books, papers and effects of every description, in his possession, belonging to said city or appertaining to his said office, he shall forfeit and pay, for the use of the city, fifty dollars, besides all damages and costs caused by his refusal or neglect so to deliver; and such successor may recover possession of the books, papers and effects belonging to his office, in the manner prescribed by the laws of the state.

§ 18. All officers elected or appointed under this act shall be commissioned by warrant, under the corporate seal, signed by the mayor or presiding officer of the city council and clerk.

Article V.

OF THE LEGISLATIVE POWERS OF THE CITY COUNCIL—ITS GENERAL POWERS AND DUTIES.

Sec. 1. City Council.
2. Meetings,
3. Finances.
First. Borrow money.
Third. Diseases.
Fourth. Health.
Fifth. Water.
Sixth. Streets, &c.
Seventh. Bridges,
Eighth. Lighting streets.
Ninth. Markets.
Tenth. Public grounds.
Twelfth. Incumbering of streets.
Thirteenth. Tax.
Fourteenth. Hackmen.
Fifteenth. Billiard Tables, &c.
Sixteenth. Licenses.
Seventeenth. Sale of intoxicating liquors.
Nineteenth. Butchers.
Twentieth. Weights and measures.
Twenty-first. Lumber, &c.
Twenty second. Hay, &c.
Twenty-third Beef, &c.
Twenty-fourth. Bread.
Twenty-fifth. Bricks.

Twenty-sixth. Police.
Twenty-seventh. Riot.
Twenty-eighth. Horse racing.
Twenty-ninth. Vagrants.
Thirtieth. Horses, &c.
Thirty-first. Unnecessary disturbance.
Thirty-second. Nuisances.
Thirty-fifth. Breweries, &c.
Thirty-sixth. Burial of dead.
Thirty-seventh. Census.
Thirty-eighth. Workhouse.
Thirty-ninth. Care of juvenile vagrants.
Fortieth. Drains. &c.
Forty-first. Railroad tracks and depots within the city. Repairing of streets.
Forty-second. Peace, trade, &c., protected by ordinance. Fines and penalties.

§ 1. The mayor and aldermen shall constitute the city council. They shall meet and organize the first Thursday after their election, and shall meet at such times and places thereafter as they shall determine. The mayor, when present, shall preside at all meetings of the city council, and shall have only a casting vote; in his absence any one of the aldermen may be appointed to preside. A majority of the persons elected [aldermen] shall constitute a quorum.

§ 2. The city council shall hold twelve stated meetings, one in each month, during the year; and the mayor or any two aldermen, may call special meetings of the council, served personally or left at their usual places of abode. Petitions and remonstrances may be presented to the city council; and they shall determine the rule of their own proceeding and be the judges of the election and qualification of their own members; and shall have power to compel the attendance of absent members.

§ 3. The city council shall have the control of the finances, and of the property, real and personal and mixed, belonging to the corporation; and shall likewise have power within the jurisdiction of the city, by ordinance,

First—To borrow money on the credit of the city, and issue bonds of the city therefor; but no bonds shall be issued having more than five years to run; and there shall never be outstanding bonds to a greater amount than two per cent. of the last assessed value of the real and personal property of the city. It shall be the duty of the council to provide, either by taxation or the issue of bonds, for the payment of all claims against the city as rapidly as such claims fall due. All orders on the treasury shall be made payable on demand. No appropriation shall be made for any public building or other improvement out of the general fund of the city, except in such cases as where the city council shall not have authority to provide for the same by special taxation levied on the property benefited thereby, or where the city council shall, by resolution, declare that it will be unjust and inequitable that the property in the vicinity shall bear the expense of such improvement, and that such improvement is required by the general interests of the city. And no appropriation shall be made for any public improvements until the expense of such improvement shall be estimated by the proper officers, and unless it shall be found, by such estimates and a statement of the estimated cost of all other public work in progress and other probable expenses of the city, that all such works can be completed within due time by the ordinary surplus revenue of the city and the issue of such bonds as the council is by law authorized to issue.

Second—To appropriate money, and to provide for the payment of the debts and expenses of the city.

Third—To make regulations to prevent the introduction of contagious diseases into the city; to make quarantine laws for that purpose, and to enforce them within the city and within five miles thereof.

Fourth—To make regulations to secure the general health and comfort of the inhabitants; to prevent, abate and remove nuisances, and punish the authors thereof by penalties, fine and imprisonment; to define and declare what shall be deemed nuisances, and to authorize and direct the summary abatement thereof.

Fifth—To provide the city with water; to make, regulate and establish public wells, pumps and cisterns by drains, hydrants and reservoirs in the streets, within the city or beyond the limits thereof, for the extinguishment of fire and the convenience of the inhabitants, and to prevent the unnecessary waste of water.

Sixth—To have the exclusive control and power over the streets, alleys and highways of the city, and to abate and remove any encroachments or obstructions thereon; to open, alter, abolish, widen, extend, straighten, establish, regulate, grade, clean, or otherwise improve the same; to put drains or sewers therein, and prevent the incumbering thereof in any manner, and protect the same from any encroachment or injury.

Seventh—To establish, erect, construct, regulate and keep

in repair, bridges, culverts and sewers, sidewalks and cross-ways, and regulate the construction and use of the same, and to abate any obstructions or encroachments thereof; to establish, alter, change and straighten the channels of water courses and natural drains, to sewer the same or to wall them up and cover them over, and to prevent, regulate and control the fitting up, altering or changing the channels thereof by private persons.

Eighth—To provide for the lighting of the streets and erecting lamp posts and lamps therein, and regulate the lighting thereof, and from time to time create, alter or extend lamp districts; to exclusively regulate, direct and control the laying and repairing of gas fixtures in the streets, alleys and sidewalks.

Ninth—To establish markets and market houses and other public buildings of the city, and provide for the government and regulation thereof, and the erection and location thereof, and to authorize their erection in the streets and avenues of the city, and the continuation of such as are already erected within the same.

Tenth—To provide for the inclosing, regulating and improving all public grounds and cemeteries, belonging to the city, and to direct and regulate the planting and preserving of ornamental and shade trees in the streets and public grounds.

Eleventh—To erect and establish one or more hospitals or dispensaries, and control and regulate the same.

Twelfth—To prevent the encumbering of the streets, alleys, sidewalks or public grounds with carriages, wagons, carts, wheelbarrows, boxes, lumber, timber, firewood, posts, awnings, signs, or any other substance or material whatever; to compel all persons to keep the snow, ice, dirt and other rubbish from the sidewalk and street gutter in front of the premises occupied by them.

Thirteenth—To license, tax and regulate merchants, commission merchants, and all venders, dealers, and traders in any goods, wares, merchandise, groceries or liquids, (alcoholic liquors excepted only, as hereinafter provided,) and innkeepers, brokers, money brokers, insurance brokers, and auctioneers, and to impose duties upon the sale of goods at auction; to license, tax, regulate, suppress and prohibit hawkers, peddlers, pawnbrokers, grocery keepers, and keepers of ordinaries, theatrical, or other exhibitions, shows and amusements: *Provided*, however, they may regulate, tax and license the keeping thereof, if a majority of the voters of the city, at the first city election, authorize them to do so, in the same manner as is provided to determine about the sale of intoxicating liquors.

Fourteenth—To license, tax, regulate and suppress hackmen, draymen, omnibus drivers, porters, and all others pursuing like occupations, with or without vehicles, and prescribe their compensation, and to regulate and restrain runners for cars, stages and public houses.

Fifteenth—To prohibit and suppress billiard tables, pin alleys and ball alleys; to suppress and restrain disorderly houses, tippling shops and groceries, bawdy houses, gaming and gambling houses, lotteries, and all fraudulent devices and practices, and all playing of cards, dice and other games of chance, with or without betting, and to authorize the destruction of all instruments and devices used for the purpose of gambling.

Sixteenth—To authorize the proper officer of the city to grant and issue licenses, and to direct the manner of issuing and registering thereof, and the fees and charges to be paid therefor. No license shall be granted for more than one year; and no license shall be granted for more than thirty days, except with power reserved to the city council to revoke such license at pleasure. The city council shall have power to regulate, license, tax, prohibit, and punish the sale of intoxicating, alcoholic or malt liquors, wine, cider, beer, soda water, or all and any drinks whatever: *Provided, however*, the said council shall have no power to authorize the sale of intoxicating liquors, except for mechanical, medicinal or religious purposes, unless the voters of the said city, shall, at their first election, to be held as hereinbefore provided, authorize, by a majority of the votes then given, the common council to authorize such sale: *And it is hereby provided*, that at the said election the poll books then used shall be provided with two columns, in one of which shall be set forth the number of votes in favor of authorizing the said council to exercise, in their discretion, the power of licensing the sale of intoxicating drinks; and on the other shall be set forth the number of votes against authorizing the said council to grant such license, as above provided. And if it shall appear that a majority of the votes polled are in favor of authorizing the common council to grant licenses, in their discretion, as aforesaid, then said council shall thenceforth have as full power as though the written proviso were not a part of this charter; but if no such majority shall appear, then the power of the common council shall thenceforth be restricted, as provided in the above written proviso.

Seventeenth—To regulate the license and tax the keeping and sale, by druggists, or other persons authorized by the city council, of alcoholic liquors, for sacramental, mechanical or medicinal purposes, but to no other persons and for no other use or purpose whatsoever, except as hereinafter provided.

Eighteenth—To prevent, restrain and punish forestalling and regrating; to regulate the inspection and vending of fresh meats, poultry and vegetables, of butter, lard and other provisions, and the place and manner of selling fish and inspecting the same.

Nineteenth—To regulate, license and prohibit butchers, and to revoke their licenses for malconduct in the course of trade.

Twentieth—To establish standard weights and measures, and regulate the weights and measures to be used within the city in all cases not otherwise provided by law; to require all traders and dealers in merchandise or property of any description, which is sold by measure or weight, to cause their measures and weights to be tested and sealed by the city sealer, and to be subject to his inspection. The standard of such weights and measures shall be conformable to those established by law and ordinance.

Twenty-first—To regulate and provide for the inspecting and measuring of lumber, shingles, timber, posts, staves, heading, and all kinds of building material, and for the measuring of all kinds of mechanical work, and to appoint one or more inspectors or measurers.

Twenty second—To provide for the inspection and weighing of hay, lime, and stone coal, and the place and manner of selling the same; to regulate the measurement of firewood, charcoal and other fuel, to be sold or used within the city, and the place and manner of selling the same.

Twenty third—To regulate the inspection of beef, pork, flour, meal and other provisions; salt, whisky and other liquors, to be sold in barrels, hogsheads and other vessels or packages; to appoint weighers, gaugers and inspectors, and prescribe their duties and regulate their fees: *Provided*, that nothing herein contained shall be so construed as to require the inspection of any articles enumerated herein, which are to be shipped beyond the limits of the state, except at the request of the owner thereof or his agent.

Twenty-fourth—To regulate the weight and quality of bread, to be sold or used within the city, and the inspection thereof.

Twenty-fifth—To regulate the size and quality of bricks to be sold or used within the city, and the inspection thereof.

Twenty-sixth—To create, establish and regulate the policy of the city; to appoint watchmen and policemen, and prescribe their duties and powers.

Twenty seventh—To prevent and suppress any riot, affray, noise, disturbance or disorderly assembly, in any public or private place within the city.

Twenty eighth—To prohibit, prevent and suppress horse-racing, immoderate riding or driving in the city, and to authorize persons immoderately riding or driving, as aforesaid, to be stopped by any person; to prohibit and punish the abuse of animals; to compel persons to fasten their horses or other animals, attached to vehicles or otherwise, while standing or remaining in the streets.

Twenty-ninth—To restrain and punish vagrants, mendicants, street beggars and prostitutes, and provide for the arrest and punishment of persons found intoxicated in the streets or public places.

Thirtieth—To regulate, restrain or prohibit the running at large of horses, cattle, asses, mules, swine, sheep, goats and geese, and to authorize the distraining, impounding and sale of the same, for the costs of the proceedings and the penalty incurred, and to impose penalties on the owners thereof for a violation of any ordinance in relation thereto; to regulate, restrain and prohibit the running at large of dogs, and to authorize their destruction when at large contrary to ordinance, and to impose penalties on the owners or keepers thereof.

Thirty-first—To prohibit and restrain the rolling of hoops, flying of kites, or any other amusements or practices tending to annoy persons passing on the streets or sidewalks, or to frighten horses or teams; to restrain and prohibit the ringing of bells, blowing of horns or bugles, crying of goods or [and] all other noises, performances and practices, tending to the collecting of persons on the streets or sidewalks, by auctioneers and others, for the purpose of business, amusement or otherwise.

Thirty-second—To abate all nuisances which may injure or affect the public morals, health or comfort, in any manner they may deem expedient.

Thirty-third—To do all acts and make all regulations which may be necessary or expedient for the protection and promotion of health, and the suppression of disease.

Thirty-fourth—To compel the owner of any grocery, cellar, soap or tallow chandler, or blacksmith shop, tanneries, stable, privy, sewer, or any other unwholesome or nauseous house or place, to cleanse, remove or abate the same as may be necessary for the health, comfort and convenience of the inhabitants.

Thirty-fifth—To direct the location and regulate the management and construction of breweries, tanneries, blacksmith shops, foundries, livery stables and packing houses; to direct the location and management and direct the construction of, and restrain, abate and prohibit, within the city, and to the distance of one mile from the limits thereof, distilleries, slaughtering establishments, establishments for [steaming or rendering lard, tallow, offal, and such other substances as may be rendered, and all other establishments or other places where any nauseous, offensive or unwholesome business may be carried on.

Thirty-sixth—To regulate the burial of dead; to establish one or more cemeteries; to regulate the registration of births and deaths; to direct the returning and keeping of bills of mortality, and to impose penalties on physicians, and sextons, and others, for any default in the premises.

Thirty seventh—To provide for the taking an enumeration of the inhabitants of the city.

Thirty-eighth—To erect and establish a workhouse or house of correction, make all necessary regulations therefor, and appoint all necessary keepers or assistants in such workhouse or house of correction, in which may be confined all vagrants, stragglers, idle and disorderly persons, who may be committed thereto by any proper officers, and all persons sentenced by any criminal court or magistrate court, in and for the city, for any assault and battery, petit larceny or other misdemeanor or breach of any ordinance of the city, punishable by imprisonment in any county jail; and any person who shall fail or neglect to pay any fine, penalty or costs imposed by any ordinance of the city, for any misdemeanor or breach of any ordinance of the city, may, instead of being committed to the county jail of Knox county, be kept therein, subject to labor and confinement.

Thirty ninth—To authorize and direct the taking up and providing for the safe keeping and education, for such periods of time as may be deemed expedient, of all children who are destitute of proper parental care.

Fortieth—To fill up, drain, cleanse, alter, relay, repair and regulate any grounds, lots, yards, cellars, private drains, sinks and privies, direct and regulate their construction, and cause the expenses thereof to be assessed and collected in the same manner as sidewalk assessments.

Forty-first—To direct and control the laying and construction of railroad tracks, bridges, turn-outs and switches, in the streets and alleys, and the location of depot grounds within the city; to require that railroad tracks, bridges, turn-outs and switches shall be so constructed and laid out as to interfere as little as possible with the ordinary travel and use of the streets and alleys, and that sufficient space shall be left on either side of said tracks for the safe and convenient passage of teams and persons; to require railroad companies to keep in repair the streets through which their tracks may run, and to construct and keep in repair suitable crossings at the intersections of streets and alleys, and sewers, and ditches, and culverts, when the city council shall deem necessary; to direct and prohibit the use and regulate the speed of locomotive engines, within the inhabited portions of the city; to prohibit and restrain railroad companies from doing storage or warehouse business, or collecting pay for storage.

Forty-second—The city council shall have power to pass, publish, amend and repeal all ordinances, rules and police regulations, not contrary to the constitution or laws of the United States or of this state, for the good government, peace and order of the city, and the trade and commerce thereof, that may be necessary or proper to carry into effect the powers vested by this act in the corporation, the city government or any department or office thereof; to determine what shall [be a] nuisance, and provide for the punishment, removal and abatement of the same; to enact and enforce the observance of all such rules, ordinances and police regulations, and to punish violations of the same by fines, penalties and imprisonment in the county jail, city prison or workhouse, or both, in the discretion of the court or magistrate before whom conviction may be had; but no fine or penalty shall exceed five hundred dollars, nor the imprisonment six months, for any offense; and such fine or penalty may be recovered, with costs, in an action for debt, in the name or for the use of the city, before any court having jurisdiction, or by presentment or indictment in the circuit court, and any person upon whom any fine or penalty is imposed, shall stand committed until the payment of the same and costs, and in a default thereof, may be imprisoned in the county jail, city prison, workhouse, or required to labor on the streets or other public works of the city, for such time and in such manner as may be provided by ordinance.

Article VI.

OF TAXATION.

First. General taxes.
Second, Road and street taxes.

§ 1. The city council shall have power, within the city, by ordinance,

First—To levy and collect, annually, [taxes] on all real and personal estate and property within the city, and all personal property of the inhabitants thereof, made taxable by the laws of the state for state purposes, to defray the general and contingent expenses of the city, not herein otherwise provided for; which taxes shall constitute the general fund.

Second—To require every male resident of the city, over the age of twenty-one years and under fifty years, to labor three days in each year upon the streets and alleys of the city; but any person may, at his option, pay, in lieu thereof, one dollar for each day required: *Provided*, the same shall be paid within ten days after notification by the street commissioner. In default of payment, as aforesaid, the sum of three dollars and costs may be collected, and no set-off shall be allowed in any suit brought to collect the same.

ARTICLE VII.

OF ASSESSMENTS FOR OPENING STREETS AND ALLEYS.

§ 1. The city council shall havepower, upon the petition of the owners of two-thirds of the property fronting thereon, and, without such petition, by the unanimous vote of the city council, to open and lay out public grounds or squares, streets, alleys and highways, or sections thereof, and to alter, widen, construct, straighten and discontinue the same; but no street, alley or highway, or any part thereof, shall be discontinued or contracted, without the consent, in writing, of all persons owning land or lots adjoining said street, alley or highway. The city council shall cause all streets, alleys and highways, or public squares or grounds, laid out by them, to be surveyed, described and recorded in a book to be kept by the clerk, showing accurately and particularly the proposed improvements, and the real estate required to be taken; and the same, when opened and made, shall be public highways and public squares.

§ 2. Whenever any street, alley or highway, public ground or square, is proposed to be laid out, opened, altered, widened or straightened, by virtue hereof, and the amount of compensation cannot be agreed upon, the city council shall give notice of their intention to appropriate and take the land necessary for the same to the owner thereof, by publishing said notice by two insertions in a weekly paper or six insertions in a daily paper, in the newspaper publishing the ordinances of the city; at the expiration of which time they shall appoint three disinterested freeholders, residing in the city, as commissioners, to ascertain and assess the damage and recompense due the owners of said real estate, respectively, and at the same time, determine what persons will be benefited by such improvement, and assess the damages and expenses thereof, on the real estate in the neighborhood of the improvement benefited thereby, in proportion, as nearly as may be, to the benefits resulting to each. A majority of the councilmen authorized by law to be elected shall be necessary to a choice of commissioners. The commissioners shall be sworn faithfully and impartially to execute their duties, to the best of their abilities, before entering upon their duties; they shall give at least five days' personal notice of the time and place of their meeting for the purposes of viewing the premises and making their assessments; which notice shall be given only to the owners who are residents thereof and known. They shall view the premises, and, in their discretion, receive any legal evidence, and may, if necessary, adjourn from day to day.

§ 3. If there should be any buildings standing, in whole or in part, upon the land to be taken, the commissioners, before proceeding to make their assessment, shall first estimate and determine the whole value of such building to the owner, aside from the value of the land, and the actual injury to him in having such building taken from him, and, secondly the value of such building to him, to remove.

§ 4. At least five days' notice shall be given to the owner, of such determination, when known and a resident of the city, which may be given personally, or in writing left at his usual place of abode. If a non resident, or unknown, like notice to all persons interested shall be given, by one publication in the newspaper publishing the ordinances of the city. Such notice shall specify the buildings and the award of the commissioners. It shall also require the person interested, to appear, by a day named therein, not exceeding thirty days, or give notice of their election to the city council, either to accept the award of the commissioners, and allow such building to be taken, with the land condemned or appropriated, or of their intention to receive such building at the value set thereon by the commissioners, to remove. If the owner shall agree to remove such building he shall have such reasonable time for that purpose as the city council may direct.

§ 5. If the owner refuses to take the building at its appraised value, to remove, or fail to give notice of his intention, as aforesaid, within the time prescribed, the city council shall have power to direct the sale of such building, at public auction, for cash, or on a credit, giving five days' public notice of the sale. The proceeds of the sale shall be paid to the owner or deposited to his use.

§ 6. In making their asessment, the said commissioners shall ascertain the value of the land taken, and all expenses of the improvement and damages occasioned thereby, and then assess upon the property in the neighborbood benefited, in fair proportions, a sum sufficient to cover the whole amount thereof; which shall be paid by the owners, respectively, and be a lien upon the property on which it may be assessed, and collected as other taxes are collected, by sale of the land or otherwise. The value of the land taken from any owner shall be a credit to him on the assessment against him for his share of the improvement; and, if more, the difference shall be paid him in money before the land is taken. Said commissioners shall particularly describe the lands and parcels on which either assessment may be made, and make a return of their proceedings and assessments to the city council, within ten days after its completion.

§ 7. The clerk shall give ten days' notice, by one publication in the newspaper publishing the ordinances of the city, that such assessment has been returned, and on the day to be specified therein will be acted upon by the city council, unless objections are made to the same by some person interested. Objections may be heard before the city council and the hearing may be adjourned from day to day. The council shall have power, in their discretion, to alter, confirm or annul the assessment. If annulled, all the proceedings shall be void. If altered or confirmed, an order shall be entered, directing a warrant to issue for the collection thereof.

§ 8. The citv council shall have power te remove the commissioners, and, from time to time, appoint others in place of such as may be removed, refuse, neglect, or are unable, from any cause, to serve.

§ 9. The land required to be taken for the making, opening, widening, straightening or altering any street, alley, or other highway or public ground, or square, shall not be appropriated until the damages awarded therefor, to any owner thereof, under this act, shall be paid or tendered to such owner, or his agent, or in case such owner or agent cannot be found in the city, deposited to his or their credit, in some safe place of deposit, other than the hands of the treasurer; and then, and not before, such lands may be taken and appropriated for the purpose required in making such improvements; and such streets, alleys, or other highways or public ground may be made and opened.

§ 10. Any person interested may appeal from any final

order of the city council for opening, widening, straightening or altering any street, alley or other highway or public ground, to the police court or circuit court. After the passage of said final order, said court to determine such appeal, and confirm or annul the proceedings; from which appeal no judgment or writ of error shall lie. Upon trial of the appeal all questions involved in said proceedings, including the amount of damages, shall be open to investigation, by affidavit or oral testimony adduced to the court; or upon applications of the city, or any party, the amount of damages may be assessed by a jury, in said court, without formal pleadings, and judgment rendered accordingly. The court shall not set aside the proceedings or final order of the council, for any omission or informality, without injury has resulted therefrom.

§ 11. When any owner known, or other person having an interest in any real estate, residing in the city or elsewhere, shall be an infant, and any proceedings shall be had under this act, the judge of the circuit court, or any judge of a court of record, may, upon the application of the city council, or such infant, or his next friend, appoint a guardian for such infant, taking security from such guardian for the faithful execution of such trust; and all notices and summons required by this act shall be served on such guardian, and the final determination of either the common council or court in the premises shall be conclusive on such infant, and the proceedings shall not be opened at any time thereafter.

Article VIII.

PUBLIC IMPROVEMENTS, AND ASSESSMENTS THEREFOR.

§ 1. The city council shall have power, from time to time, upon the petition of the owners of two-thirds of the property fronting thereon, or without such petition, by the unanimous vote of the council, to cause any street, alley or other highways or sections thereof, to be graded, regraded, levelled, paved or planked, and keep the same in repair, and alter and change the same; to cause side and cross walks, main drains and sewers, and private drains or sections thereof, to be constructed and laid, relaid, cleansed and repaired, and regulate the same; to grade, improve, protect and ornament any public square or other public ground now or hereafter laid out.

§ 2. The city council shall have power to assess and collect of the owners of lots or real estate on any street or other highway, or any part thereof, in the same manner as other city taxes, or in such a manner as may be prescribed by ordinance, all expenses and damages for the purpose of grading, paving or planking such street, sidewalk, pavement or other highway. All owners or occupants of lots or lands in front of, or adjoining, or upon whose premises the city council shall order and direct sidewalks or private drains or gutters, communicating with any main drain, to be constructed, graded, paved, planked, repaired, relaid or cleansed, or shall declare any such lands or lots to be nuisances, and order the same to be graded, filled up and drained, or otherwise improved, shall make, grade, pave, plank, repair or relay such sidewalk, or make or cleanse such private drain, or grade, fill up, drain or otherwise improve such lot or land, at their own cost and charges, within the time and in manner prescribed by ordinance or otherwise, and if not done within the time and in the manner prescribed, the city council may cause the same to be constructed, paved, planked, repaired, relaid, cleansed, filled up, graded, drained or otherwise improved, and assess the expense and damage thereof, by an order to be entered in their proceedings, upon the lots and lands respectively, and collect the same, by warrant and sale of the premises, as in other cases. A suit may also be maintained against the owner of such premises, for the recovery of such expenses, as for money paid and laid out to his use at his request.

§ 3. In all cases where expenses may be incurred in the removal of any nuisance, the city council may cause the same to be assessed against the real estate chargeable therewith, in the same manner prescribed in the foregoing section. Such expenses may be likewise collected by the owner or occupant of such premises, in a suit for money expended to his or their use; and in case the same should not be chargeable to any real estate, suit may in like manner be brought for such expenses against the author of such nuisances, if known, or any person whose duty may be to remove or abate the same.

§ 4. The city council shall have power to compel the owners of lots or ground fronting or adjoining any public or private alley to keep the same clean, and, if necessary, to direct the same to be paved, planked or otherwise, and the costs thereof to be assessed and collected in the same manner as sidewalk assessments.

ARTICLE IX.

COLLECTION OF TAXES, AND ASSESSMENTS.

SECTION 2. Assessment list to be filed.
4. Warrants for taxes.
6. Treasurer to have the powers of county collectors.
9. Manner of conducting sales.
10. Right of redemption.
11. Assignees.

§ 1. The annual assessment lists shall be returned by the assessor, on or before the first day in August in each year; but the time may be extended by the city council. On the return thereof the city council shall fix a day for hearing objections thereto; and the clerk shall give one weeks' notice of the time and place of such hearing, by one publication in the newspaper publishing the ordinances of the city; and any person feeling agrieved by the assessment of his property, may appear, at the time specified, and make his objections. The city council shall have power to supply omissions in said assessment lists, and, for the purpose of equalizing the same, to alter, add to, take from, and otherwise correct and revise the same, or to refer the same back to the assessors, with instructions to revise and correct the same; and the treasurer shall have power to add to and supply omissions by the assessor, after the warrant shall have come into his hands.

§ 2. When the assessment lists have been corrected and revised, the same shall be filed, and an order confirming the same and directing the warrant to be issued for the collection thereof shall be entered by the clerk. The city council shall, thereupon, by an ordinance or resolution, levy such sum or sums of money as may be sufficient for the several purposes, for which taxes are herein authorized to be levied, not exceeding the authorized per centage, and in their discretion specifying the purposes for which the same are levied, and, if not for general purposes, the division of the city upon which the same are laid.

§ 3. All taxes and assessments, general or special, levied or assessed by the city council, under this act, or any ordinance in pursuance thereof, shall be a lien upon the real estate upon which the same may be imposed, voted or assessed, for two years from and after said first day of August, and on personal estate from and after the delivery of the warrant for the collection thereof, until paid; and no sale or transfer shall affect the lien. Any personal property belonging to the debtor may be taken and sold for the payment of taxes on real estate, [and the real estate] shall be liable for taxes on personal estate in case of removal: *Provided*, that in case the collection of any assessment shall be delayed by injunction or other judicial proceedings, the same shall continue a lien, unless set aside, upon the real estate, for the period of two years from and after the final disposition of such injunction or other judicial proceeding.

§ 4. The clerk shall issue a warrant or warrants for the taxes, and rule therein separate columns, in which the taxes levied shall be respectively set down opposite the name of the person or such real estate subject thereto. Each column shall be headed with the name of the tax therein set down.

§ 5. All warrants issued for the collection of general or special taxes and assessments shall be signed by the mayor and clerk, with the corporate seal thereto attached, and shall contain true and perfect copies of the corrected assessment lists upon which the same may be collected, and shall be delivered to the treasurer for collection, by the first day of October, unless further time be given by the city council, of which he shall give notice, by publication in the newspaper publishing the city ordinances. The treasurer shall, thereupon, proceed to the collection of said taxes; but he shall in no case be compelled to make personal call or demand for the same. If not otherwise paid by the first day of January following, the treasurer shall have power to collect said taxes, with interest and costs, by suit, in the corporate name of the city, or by distress and sale of personal property. And the treasurer shall be a competent witness, and the warrant to him, as aforesaid, evidence on the part of said city.

§ 6. All taxes or assessments, general or special, shall be collected by the treasurer, in the same manner, and with the same power and authority, as is given by law to collectors of county and state taxes; and his duty in regard to returning warrants and settling with the city, and his liabilities in case of default or misconduct, shall be the same as prescribed by law: *Provided*, the city council shall have power to prescribe the powers, duties and liabilities of the treasurer by ordinance.

§ 7. In case of the non-payment of any taxes or assessments, levied or assessed under this act, by the first day of January of each year, the premises may be sold, at any time thereafter, within two years. Before such sale an order shall be made by the city council, which shall be entered at large on the journals or records, particularly describing the delinquent premises to be sold, and the amount of taxes for which the sale shall be made, besides the costs, which costs need not then be ascertained, and directing sale thereby to be made by the treasurer; a certified copy of which order, under the corporate seal, signed by the mayor or presiding officer and clerk; shall be delivered to the treasurer, and shall constitute the process upon which such sale shall be made.

§ 8. The treasurer shall then advertise such premises, in the newspaper publishing the ordinances of the city, for sale, at least thirty days from and after the first publication of such notice, describing the premises, by figures or otherwise, with the name of the owner, when known, and the several amounts of the taxes and assessments thereon, and costs. Said notice shall also contain the time and place of sale, and shall be published at least four times. The proceedings for the sale of any piece of ground may be stopped, at any time, on the payment of taxes and interest, with expense of advertising the same.

§ 9. All sales shall be conducted in the manner required by law; but the city council shall have the power to prescribe the manner of conducting the same. The sale shall be made for the smallest portion of ground, to be taken from the east side of the premises, for which any person will take the same and pay the taxes or assessments thereon, with interest and costs of sale. Duplicate certificates of sale shall be made and subscribed by the treasurer, one of which shall be delivered to the purchaser, and the other filed in the office of the clerk; which certificate shall contain the name of the purchaser, a description of the premises sold, the amount of taxes or assessments, with the interest and expenses for which the same was sold, and when the time to redeem will expire. The treasurer will be allowed the same fees for selling as are allowed by law for similar services, or his fee may be regulated by ordinance. The clerk shall keep a record of such sales, which shall be open to the public inspection at all reasonable times.

§ 10. The right of redemption, in all cases for sales for taxes or assessments, shall exist to the owner, his heirs, creditors or assigns, to the same extent that it is allowed by law in cases of sales of real estate for taxes, on the payment, in specie, of double the amount for which the same was sold; and all taxes accruing, chargeable or paid on the premises, subsequent to the sale, with interest; but infants, *femme coverts* or lunatics shall have no other or further rights of redemption than other persons. In case of redemption, the money may be paid to the purchaser or to the person entitled to the same, or for him to the city clerk, who shall make a special deposit thereof with the treasurer, taking his receipt therefor. If not redeemed according to law, the city council shall, upon the return of the certificate, or proof of its loss, direct a deed to be executed to the purchaser, under the corporate seal, signed by the mayor or presiding officer of the city council, and countersigned by the clerk, conveying to such purchaser the premises so sold and unredeemed as aforesaid. An abstract of all deeds so made and delivered shall be entered by the clerk in a book wherein tax sales are recorded. A fee of one dollar may be charged by the clerk for any deed so issued.

§ 11. The assignee of any tax certificate of any premises sold fer taxes or assessments, under authority of the city, shall be entitled to receive a deed of such premises, in his own name, and with the same effect as though he had been the original purchaser, *provided*, he or they through whom he claims shall have paid all taxes and assessments made since said sale, on said premises.

§ 12. If at any sale of real or personal estate, for taxes or assessments, no bids shall be made for any parcel of land, or any goods and chattels, the same shall be struck off to the city, and thereupon the city shall receive, in the corporate name, a certificate of the sale thereof, and shall be vested with the same rights as other purchasers at such sales. All persons, before they shall be entitled to a deed for premises sold for the non-payment of taxes, shall comply with sec. 4, article 9, of the constitution of this state, and shall produce to the proper officers the proof thereof.

§ 13. All sales of lands or lots for non-payment of taxes contemplated by this act, and deeds made to purchasers or their assigns for the same, shall convey to the holder of such deed a perfect title in fee simple to said land or lot, and in all suits and controversies in relation thereto, any person claiming such title shall be compelled to prove only the order of the city council directing the sale, and the process upon which the sale was made, as provided for in section seven of article nine of this act; and any person claiming title adversely thereto, shall be permitted to defeat such title by proving that such land or lot was not subject to taxation at the time of the assessment, or that the taxes were paid, or land or lot redeemed according to the provisions of this act; but no person shall be permitted to question the title acquired by said deed, without first showing that he or they, or those under whom he or they claim, have paid the full amount of taxes, costs, expenses and assessments made on said land or lot since said sale for taxes, or that the same has been deposited with the city treasurer for the use of the one entitled to receive it.

Article X.

FIRE DEPARTMENT.

§ 1. The city council, for the purpose of guarding against the calamities of fire, shall have power to prohibit the erection, placing or repairing of wooden buildings, within the limits prescribed by them, without their permission, and direct and prescribe that all buildings within the limits prescribed, shall be made or constructed of fire-proof materials, and to prohibit the rebuilding of wooden buildings; to declare all dilapidated buildings to be nuisances, and direct the same to be repaired, removed or abated in such manner as they shall prescribe and direct; to declare all wooden buildings which they may deem dangerous to contiguous buildings, or in causing or promoting fires, to be nuisances, and require and cause the same to be removed or abated in such a manner as they shall prescribe.

§ 2. The city council shall have power,

First—To regulate the construction of chimneys and flues, so as to admit of chimney sweeps or other mode of cleaning, and to compel the sweeping and cleaning of chimneys.

Second—To prevent and prohibit the dangerous construction of chimneys, flues, fire places, stovepipes, ovens or any other apparatus, used in or about any building or manufactory, and to cause the same to be removed or placed in a secure and safe condition, when considered dangerous.

Third—To prevent the deposit of ashes in unsafe places, and to appoint one or more officers to enter into all buildings and enclosures, to examine and discover whether the same are in a dangerous state, and to cause such as are dangerous to be put in a safe condition.

Fourth—To require the inhabitants to provide as many fire buckets, and in such manner and time as they shall prescribe, and to regulate the use thereof in times of fire; and to require all owners and occupants of buildings to construct and keep in repair wells or cisterns upon their premises.

Fifth—To regulate and prevent the carrying on of manufactories and works dangerous in promoting and causing fires.

Sixth—To regulate, prevent and prohibit the use of fire works and fire arms.

Seventh—To prohibit or have the management of houses for storing of gunpowder, or direct and prohibit other and dangerous materials within the city, to regulate the keeping and conveying of the same, and the use of candles and other lights in stables and other like houses.

Eighth—To regulate and prescribe the manner and order the building of parapets and walls, and of partition fences.

Ninth—To compel the owners or occupants of houses or other buildings to have scuttles in the roofs, and stairs or ladders leading to the same.

Tenth—To authorize the mayor, fire wardens or other officers of the said city to keep away from the fire all and any suspicious persons, and to compel all officers of the city and all other persons to aid in the extinguishment of fire, and in the preservation of property exposed to damage or danger thereat, and in preventing goods from being stolen.

Eleventh—And, generally, to establish such regulations for the prevention and extinguishment of fires, as the city council may deem expedient.

§ 3. The city council may procure fire engines and all other apparatus used or the extinguishment of fires, and have the charge and control of the same, and provide secure and fit houses and other places for keeping and preserving the same; and shall have power,

First—[To] organize fire, hook, hose, axe and ladder companies.

Second—To appoint, during their pleasure, a competent number of able and reputable inhabitants of the city, firemen, to take the care and management of the engines and other apparatus and implements used and provided for the extinguishment of fires.

Third—To prescribe the duty of firemen; and to make rules and regulations for their government, and to impose reasonable penalties upon them for a violation of the same, and for incapacity, neglect of duty or misconduct to remove them.

Fourth—The city council shall have power to appoint a chief and assistant engineers of the fire department, and they, with the other firemen, shall take the care and management of the engines and other apparatus and implements provided and used for the extinguishment of fires, and their powers and duties shall be prescribed and defined by the city council.

Article XI.

BOARD OF HEALTH.

§ 1. The board of health shall consist of three or more commissioners, to be appointed annually by the city council; and the mayor or the presiding officer of the city council shall be president of the board; and the city clerk shall be their clerk, and keep minutes of their proceedings.

§ 2. It shall be the duty of health officers to visit every sick person, who may be reported to them, as hereinafter provided, and to report, with all convenient speed, their opinion of the sickness of such person to the clerk of the board, and to visit and inspect all houses or places in which they may suspect any person to be confined with any pestilential or infectious disease, or to contain unsound provisions or damaged or putrid animal or vegetable matter, or other unwholesome articles, and to make report of the state of the same, with all convenient speed, to the clerk of the board.

§ 3. All persons in the city, not residents thereof, who may be infected with any pestilential or infectious disorder, or all things, which, in the opinion of the board, shall be infected by or tainted with pestilential matter and ought to be removed, so as not to endanger the health of the city, shall, by order of said board, be removed to some proper place, not exceeding five miles beyond the limits of the city, to be provided by the board, at the expense of the person to be removed, if able; and the board may order any furniture or wearing apparel to be destroyed, whenever they may deem it necessary for the health of the city, by making just compensation.

§ 4. The city council shall have power to prescribe the powers and duties of the board of health, and to punish, by fine or imprisonment, or both, any refusal or neglect to observe the orders and regulations of the board.

§ 5. The health officers may be authorized by the city council, when the public interests require, to exercise, for the time being, such of the powers and perform such of the duties of marshal or street commissioner as the city council may, in their discretion, direct, and shall be authorized to enter all houses and other places, private or public, at all times, in discharge of any duty under this act or any ordinance.

§ 6. Every person practicing physic in this city, who shall have a patient laboring under any malignant, infectious or pestilential disease, shall forthwith make report thereof in writing, to the clerk of the board, and for neglect to do so shall be considered guilty of a misdemeanor, and liable to a fine of fifty dollars, to be sued for and recovered, with costs, in an action of debt, in any court having cognizance thereof, or before a justice of the peace, for the use of said city.

Article XII.

MISCELLANEOUS PROVISIONS.

§ 1. The city council shall, at least ten days before the annual election, in each year, cause to be published in the newspaper publishing the ordinances of the city, a correct and full statement of the receipts and expenditures, from the date of the last annual report, together with the sources from which the former are derived and the mode of disbursement, and also a distinct statement of the whole amount assessed, received and expended in the respctive wards and divisions, for making and repairing streets, highways and bridges, for the same period; together with such information as may be necessary to a full understanding of the financial concerns of the city.

§ 2. The inhabitants of the city of Galesburg are hereby exempted from working upon any road or highway beyond the limits of the city, and from paying the tax in lieu thereof, without said limits.

§ 3. The street commissioner shall demand the services of all persons who are required to labor on the streets and alleys of the city, at such time and in such manner as the city council may direct or the street commissioner shall deem necessary. He shall deliver or cause to be delivered or left at the usual place of abode or business of any person so required to labor, as aforesaid, a written or printed notice, or partly written or printed notice, in such form as the city council shall prescribe, which notice shall be given at least five days previous to the first day on which he or they are required to labor, requiring such person to appear at such time and place as may be designated for the purpose of laboring upon the street and alleys; but similar notice, published for ten days in the newspaper publishing the ordinances of the city, by the street commissioner, or posted up in three of the public places of the ward or district, shall be deemed sufficient notice to require all persons to appear and labor as aforesaid. Upon the neglect of any person to appear and labor as aforesaid, or to pay the tax in lieu thereof, the collector shall collect of each person, in the same manner as other taxes, the sum of three dollars, with his commission for collecting the same added thereto, or the same may be recovered by suit, with costs, as in other cases.

§ 4. The city council may provide for the payment of the city attorney's and prison keeper's fees, when they cannot be collected from the offender; but said city, or any person prosecuting on her behalf, shall not, in any case be compelled to pay or give security for costs, before commencing proceedings, nor at any other time until it is ascertained they cannot be made out of the defendant.

§ 5. All fines, forfeitures and penalties, collected for offences committed within said city, shall belong to said city, and shall be paid into the treasury thereof by officers collecting the same.

§ 6. The water course known as Cedar Fork, in said city,

or natural branch thereto, shall not be altered, filled or changed, except in the manner prescribed by the city council; and the city council shall have power to establish and direct and prescribe the manner of altering, changing, straightening, and to wall, fill up, culvert or sewer the same.

§ 7. The city council shall have power to cause the lots and blocks of the city to be surveyed, platted and numbered in consecutive numbers, from one upwards, and to designate and number all fractional or other lots or blocks, in such manner as may be prescribed by ordinance; and such plat, designation and numbers, when made and duly recorded, shall be a good and valid description of said blocks, lots or fractional blocks; to establish, mark and declare the boundaries and names of streets and alleys; to require that all additions hereafter made to said city, or all lands adjoining or within the same, laid out into blocks or lots, shall be so laid out and platted to correspond and conform to the regular blocks, streets and alleys already laid out and established within the city.

§ 9. The street commissioner, in addition to the penalties prescribed by ordinance, shall, for willful neglect of duty, be liable to indictment and fine.

§ 9. Neither the city council or mayor shall remit any fine or penalty imposed for any violation of any of the laws or ordinances of said city, or release from confinement, unless two-thirds of all the aldermen elected shall vote for such release or remission, nor shall anything in this act be so construed as to oust any court of jurisdiction to abate and remove any nuisance within its jurisdiction, by indictment or otherwise.

§ 10. No vote of the city council shall be reconsidered or rescinded at a special meeting, unless the meeting be called, in whole or in part, for that purpose, and the aldermen be so notified, and unless at such special meeting there be present as large a number of aldermen as was present when the vote was taken.

§ 11. The cemetery lots which may be laid out and sold by the city or private persons, for private places of burial, shall, with the appurtanances, forever be exempt from execution and attachment.

§ 12. Every ordinance, regulation and by-law imposing any penalty, fine, imprisonment or forfeiture, for a violation of its provisions, shall, after the passage thereof, be published three days, when there is a daily paper published in said city, otherwise, once in a weekly paper: *Provided*, the proof of such publication shall not be necessary, unless it is denied under oath; and such publication may be dispensed with entirely in cases of emergency, by the unanimous vote of the council; and proof of such publication, by the affidavit of the printer or publisher of such newspaper, taken before any officer authorized to administer oaths, and filed with the clerk, or any other competent proof of such publication, shall be conclusive evidence of the legal publication and promulgation of such ordinance, regulation or by–law, in all courts and places.

§ 13. All actions brought to recover any penalty or forfeiture incurred under this act, or any ordinance, by-law, or police regulation, made in pursuance thereof, may be brought in the corporate name. It shall be lawful to declare, generally, in debt, for such penalty, fine or forfeiture, stating the clause of this act or the by-law or ordinance under which the penalty or forfeiture is claimed, and to give the special matter in evidence under it; or the defendant may be tried by presentment in the court of common pleas.

§ 14. In all prosecutions for any violation of any ordinance, by-law or other regulation, the first process shall be a summons, unless oath or affirmation be made for warrant, as in other cases; and the council may provide for issuing the warrant, in the instance, without oath.

§ 15. The city council shall have power to designate one or more justices of the peace or police magistrates in said city, who shall have jurisdiction in any actions for the recovery of any fine, penalty or forfeiture under this act, or any ordinance, by-law or police regulation, anything in the laws of this State to the contrary notwithstanding. Such justice shall have power to impose fines and penalties, not exceeding the amount authorized by the constitution of the State.

§ 16. Execution may issue immediately on rendition of judgment; and the same execution shall require, that if the defendant has no goods or chattels or real estate within the county of Knox, whereof the judgment can be collected, that the defendant be arrested and confined in the county jail or workhouse or city prison, for a term not exceeding six months, as the council, by ordinance, may determine. And all persons who shall be committed under this section shall be confined one day for each one dollar of such judgment and costs, all expenses incurred in the prosecution for the recovery of any fine, penalty or forfeiture, when collected and paid into the city treasury.

§ 17. Any person who shall destroy or injure any bridge or any public building or any other property belonging to the city, or shall cause or procure the same to be injured, shall be subject to a penalty, not exceeding five hundred dollars, for such offense, and may be imprisoned, not exceeding six months, in the discretion of the court before whom such conviction may be had, and such person shall also be liable in a civil action, at the suit of the city or any person injured thereby, for the damages occasioned by such injury or destruction.

§ 18. No person shall be an incompetent judge, justice, witness or juror, by reason of his being an inhabitant or freeholder in said city of Galesburg, in any action or proceeding in which the said city may be a party in interest.

§ 19. All ordinances, regulations and resolutions now in force in the town of Galesburg, and not inconsistent with this act, shall remain in force, under this act, until altered, modified or repealed by the city council, after this act shall take effect.

§ 20. All rights, actions, fines, penalties and forfeitures, in suit or otherwise, which have accrued, shall be vested in and prosecuted by the corporation hereby created.

§ 21. All property, real or personal, or mixed, belonging to the town of Galesburg, is hereby vested in the corporation created by this act; and the officers of said corporation now in office shall respectively continue in the same until superseded in conformity to the provisions hereof, but shall be governed by this act; which shall take effect from and after its passage and publication in Galesburg.

§ 22. All ordinances of the city, when printed and published by authority of the city council, shall be received in all courts and places, without further proof thereof, which shall not be required until denied under oath.

§ 23. The style of all ordinances shall be: "*Be it ordained by the city council of the city of Galesburg.*"

§ 24. Any tract of land adjoining said city which may be laid out into blocks or lots and duly platted, according to law, and any tract of land adjoining the city, with the consent of the owner thereof, shall and may be annexed to said city and form a part thereof, and the city council shall have power, upon petition of the owner of the property, to reduce the boundaries of the city, not exceeding one-half mile, in any direction.

§ 25. This act shall not invalidate any legal act done by the president and trustees of Galesburg, or by its officers, nor divest their successors under this act of any rights of property, or otherwise, or liability which may have accrued to or been created by said corporation prior to the passage of this act.

§ 26. All officers of the city, created conservators of the peace by this act or authorized by any ordinance, shall have power to arrest or cause to be arrested, with or without process, all persons who shall break the peace, or threaten to break the peace, or be found violating any ordinance of this city, commit for examination, and, if necessary, detain such person in custody over night or the Sabbath, in the watch-house or other safe place, or until they can be brought before a magistrate; and shall have and exercise such other powers, as conservators of the peace, as the city council may prescribe.

§ 27. There shall be a digest of the ordinances of the city which are of a general nature published within one year after the passage of this act, and a like digest within every period of five years thereafter.

Sec. 28. This act shall be deemed a public act, and may be read in evidence, without proof, and judicial notice shall be taken thereof in all courts and places, and shall take effect from and after its passage and publication in Galesburg; there being sufficient emergency, in the judgment of the legislature, to dispense with the lapse of sixty days, before this act goes into effect.

Sec. 29. The act entitled "An act for the better government of towns and cities, and to amend the charters thereof," approved February 27, 1854, shall be constituted a part of this charter of the city of Galesburg, the same as if specially recited, except that there shall be allowed to said city two police magistrates, and that their jurisdiction shall extend to all causes of action at common law or by statute, where the plaintiff's demand shall not exceed five hundred dollars, and to all cases of misdemeanor committed within the city limits of said city, where indictment is not necessary to a conviction.

Approved, Feb. 14, 1857.

AMENDMENT

TO

CITY CHARTER.

An Act to amend the Act entitled "An Act to incorporate the City of Galesburg," Approved February 14th, 1857.

SEC. 1. Be it enacted by the people of the State of Illinois, represented in the General Assembly, that the proviso in paragraph thirteen in section three of article five of the act entitled "An act to incorporate the city of Galesburg," approved 14th February, 1857, be and the same is hereby repealed, and the city council of said city shall have full power to license, tax, regulate, or prohibit and suppress the several pursuits and business therein mentioned, as though no such were therein contained.

SEC. 2. That article seven of said Act be and the same is hereby amended so that in all cases of estimating damages occasioned by the opening or laying out of public grounds or squares, streets, alleys or highways or sections thereof in said city of Galesburg; or for altering, widening, constructing, straightening or discontinuing the same, it shall be lawful to take into consideration the benefits resulting therefrom to the owner of any land, taken or affected by such improvement, and instead of paying to him the value of the land taken for the improvement in money, he shall be entitled only to the value of such land after deducting therefrom the value of such improvement to him or his property remaining in the neighborhood.

WM. R. MORRISON,
Speaker of the House of Representatives.
JOHN WOOD,
Speaker of Senate.

Approved Feb. 19th; 1859:
WM. H. BISSELL.

AN ACT

FOR THE ESTABLISHMENT OF

A SYSTEM OF GRADED SCHOOLS,

IN THE

CITY OF GALESBURG.

SEC. 1. *Be it enacted by the People of the State of Illinois, represented in the General Assembly,*

That all the territory within the limits of the city of Galesburg, Knox County, Illinois, according to its present or future boundaries, is hereby erected into a Common School District, to be known as Galesburg School District.

SEC. 2. All school lands, school funds and other real or personal estate, notes, bonds, or other obligations, belonging to Township number eleven, north, and Range one, east of the fourth principal meridian, Knox County, Illinois, held or owned for school purposes, shall be divided between the city of Galesburg and the portion of the Township without the same, in the proportion and manner following:

The School Trustees for said Township shall, within thirty days after the first election contemplated by this act, appoint two commissioners who are free holders, one a resident of said city, the other of said township without the city; who, after being sworn well and truly to discharge their duties, shall ascertain the whole number of white persons under the age of twenty-one years, residing in the whole of said township, and the whole number in said city, and in the township without the city; and thereupon said trustees shall divide and apportion said funds, real and personal estate, notes, bonds and obligations of said township, between the city and the township without the city, according to the number of white persons under the age of twenty-one years residing in said township. Said trustees shall have power to supply any vacancy occurring among said Commissioners.

§ 3. Said trustees or other person or persons having custody or control of said funds or lands, shall pay over and deliver to the Board of Education of Galesburg School District, the portion of the funds and other personal estate, notes, bonds and obligations, to which the School District may be entitled, and execute and deliver to the Board of Education the necessary deeds and other conveyances for the sale of real estate due said District under said division.

SEC. 4. The public schools of said district shall be under the exclusive management and control of a Board of Education, to consist of the Mayor of said city, who shall be the President of the Board and one Director from each ward of the city, to be known as "the Board of Education of Galesburg School District," each of whom with the Treasurer and Clerk of said Board, shall be sworn to discharge their duties with fidelity.

SEC. 5. Said Board shall have exclusive control over the school lands, funds, and other means of said district for school purposes, and shall have full power to do all acts and things in relation thereto, to promote the end herein designed; may sell or lease said lands and other lands or property which may have been or may hereafter be donated, purchased or designed for school purposes in said district, on such terms for cash or credit, and such time as they may see proper. They shall have full power to receive conveyances or donations, and to make the necessary deeds or leases for lands; and all conveyances by the Board shall be signed and acknowledged before some competent officer by the president and secretary of said Board; provided, however, that no sale or lease of land for more than one year shall be made without the concurrence of five members of the Board. A majority of the Directors, with or without the President, shall constitute a quorum for the transaction of business, and in the absence of the President they may appoint one of their own body President *pro tempore.* The President shall only vote in case of a tie, when he shall have a casting vote.

§ 6. Said Board shall have full power to purchase or lease sites for school houses, with the necessary grounds therefor. To erect, hire, or purchase buildings for School Houses, and keep them in repair. To furnish Schools with necessary books, fixtures, furniture, apparatus and library or libraries. To establish, conduct and maintain a system of public graded schools, to be kept in one or more buildings in said district. To supply the insufficiency of school funds for the payment of teachers and other school purposes, and expenses, by school taxes, to be levied and collected as hereinafter provided. To determine the number, make the appointment, and fix the amount of compensation of teachers within said district, and of all other agents and servants; provided that the Directors shall, in no case, receive any compensation for services as Directors. To prescribe the studies to be taught, and books to be used in said school, including maps, charts, globes, &c. To lay off and divide said district into smaller districts, and to alter the same, or erect new ones at pleasure. To pass by-laws, rules and regulations to carry their powers into complete execution, and for the government of their own body, their officers, agents and servants, and providing for their meetings and adjournments; and generally, to have and possess all the rights, power and authority necessary for the proper establishment and control of an effective system of graded schools within said district. And they shall visit and inspect each and all the schools therein, as often as may be necessary.

§ 7. It shall be the duty of the Board of Education, and they shall have full power to determine the amount of money needed, and to be raised for school purposes, over and above the amount from the school funds hereinbefore enumerated, or from other sources. Provided, said Board shall not for any one year require to be raised more than one half of one per centum, for the benefit of said schools, on the assessed value of the real and personal property of said City for such year, without a majority of the voters of said City authorize them to do so, at an election to be held for that purpose, at such time and conducted in such manner as the Board may direct; nor shall said Board or said City Council make any loan whatsoever for school purposes without a previous authority by such vote, but with the concurrence of a majority of said voters, it shall be lawful to raise such sum either by taxation or loan, as said Board may see proper; and before the first day of August of each year, they shall determine the amount required to be collected by taxation for expenditure for one year from the first day of January then next ensuing, for school purposes generally, and certify the amount to the City Council of Galesburg.

§ 8. It shall thereupon be the duty of the City Council to levy said sum on all the real estate and personal property of said City, according to the assessment and valuation thereof, for the current year, equally by a certain rate per centum, and collect the same as City taxes are collected. A special column shall be prepared in the City duplicate, headed "School purposes," in which shall appear the amount of tax for school purposes chargeable against each parcel of real estate or amount of personal property, and when said taxes are collected, the Treasurer shall keep a separate account of the same, and they shall be used and applied for school purposes only, and shall be paid only on the order of said Board.

§ 9. It shall be the duty of the Board to cause an abstract of the whole number of white children under the age of twent-yone years within said district, to be made, and furnish the same, with such further information as is required in sections 36, and 79, of the act to establish and maintain a system of free schools, approved February 16th, 1847, to the School Commissioner of Knox County, Illinois, within ten days after the same shall have been ascertained, and the School Commissioner shall pay annually to the said Board for the exclusive use of said district, the amount the district is entitled to receive from the funds that are or may be in his hands, subject to distribution for the support and benefit of the schools in said County, in accordance with the provisions of the Free School Law now in force, the same as if no special charter had been conferred upon the schools of the City of Galesburg.

§ 10. The city council of the city of Galesburg are hereby vested with full power to borrow such sums of money, being subject to the restriction contained in the seventh section of this act, as they may deem necessary for school purposes in said district, at a rate of interest not exceeding ten per centum per annum, which may be made payable semi-annually at such place as may be agreed upon, and the money when so borrowed shall be placed under the control of the Board of Education.

§ 11. The Board of Education shall be elected by all the qualified voters of said School District, but one Director shall reside in each of the wards of said city, and be a householder and free-holder thereof. The Directors shall hold their offices three years from the day of their election, except that one-third of the first Board elected under this act shall retire from office at the expiration of the first year, one third at the expiration of the second year, and one third at the expiration of the third year; and the period of their retirement shall be decided as follows: The clerk of the city council shall take six strips of paper, on two of which he shall write the words "one year," on two, "two years," on two, "three years," each member elect shall draw, and shall serve the period of time indicated by the words on the paper which he draws.

An election shall be held annually at the place where the city council of Galesburg hold their meetings, on the first Monday of June, at the first of which all of said directors shall be chosen, and at each election thereafter, successors to the Directors whose terms are about to expire. For the first election, the election officers shall be appointed by the city council of Galesburg, notice thereof being published by said council ten days before the election, in a newspaper of said city, but for each subsequent election said appointment shall be made by the Board of Education, and notice given by them as aforesaid, and for what wards Directors are to be chosen; and said election shall in every other particular—the supplying vacancies in the officers thereof, substituting the place for holding the election, conducting the election, making the returns, &c., &c., be governed by the ordinance of the city of Galesburg in force at the time of election. Said Board shall be the judges of the election and qualification of its members, and in determining the same shall be governed by the city ordinance as aforesaid.

All officers under this act shall hold their offices until the election and qualification of their successors. Removal from his ward, and not out of the city, by any Director, shall not vacate his office, and whenever any vacancy shall occur in the office of Director, the city council of Galesburg shall supply the same upon notice thereof by the Board of Education; but such appointment so made by the city council shall only continue until the next regular election of Directors, when a successor shall be elected, who shall hold his office for the unexpired term only.

§ 12. The treasurer and clerk of the city of Galesburg shall be the treasurer and clerk of the Board of Education, and the Board shall determine their duties, compensation and amount of security to be given.

§ 13. Said Board shall cause all funds not needed for immediate use, to be loaned at the rate of ten per cent. per annum, payable semi-annually in advance. No loan shall be for a longer period than five years, and if exceeding one hundred dollars, shall be secured by unencumbered real estate of at least double the value of the loan, without estimating perishable improvements. For any sum of one hundred dollars and under, good and satisfactory personal security may be taken.

§ 14. All notes and securities shall be to the Board of Education, for school purposes, and the borrower shall be at all expenses of examining titles, preparing and recording papers.

§ 15. In settling the estates of deceased persons, debts for school purposes shall be preferred to all others, except those attending the last illness of the deceased, and his funeral expenses, including the physician's bill.

§ 16 If default be made in the payment of interest, or of the principal when due, interest at the rate of twelve per cent. per annum on the amount due shall be charged, from the default, and may be recovered by suit. Suit may be for the interest only, whether the principal be due or not; and if the interest be not paid within ten days after the same becomes due, the principal at the option of the holder of the note shall thereby become due, and may be recovered by suit if necessary.

§ 17. All judgments for principal or interest, or both, shall draw interest at the rate of twelve per cent. from the rendition of judgment, and said Board may purchase in property sold on execution or decree in their own favor, as other persons, with right of redemption, as in other cases. No judgment for costs shall be rendered against said Board, to be paid out of the school funds.

§ 18. If the security for any loan or other debt due the school district, in the judgment of the Board become doubtful or insecure, they shall cause the debtor to be notified thereof, and if he shall not immediately secure the same to the satisfaction of the Board, the principal and interest shall thereby become due immediately, and suit may be brought against all the makers of the note, although such condition or stipulation be not inserted in the note.

§ 19. Said Board of Education shall publish annually a statement of the number of the pupils instructed the preceding year, the several branches of education pursued, the receipts and expenditures of each school, specifying the sources of such receipts, and the objects of such expenditures.

§ 20. Said Board shall have full power to admit persons who do not reside within said district into said school, upon such terms as they may think proper.

§ 21. All free white persons, over the age of five years and under the age of twenty-one years, residing within said district, shall be admitted to said schools free, or upon the payment of such rates of tuition as the Board shall prescribe; but nothing herein contained shall prevent persons being suspended, expelled or kept out of said school altogether, for improper conduct.

§ 22. In purchasing or leasing grounds or buildings for school purposes, said Board of Education may do so on credit, and "when the price and conditions of the purchase or lease is agreed upon, the Board may certify the same to the city council of Galesburg, and the council shall make or cause to be made to the proper party the bonds or obligations of said city for the payment of the purchase money according to said terms, or said Board may execute in their own name said contract, bonds or obligations, and they shall be binding upon said city; and the council shall provide for the payment of the same, and the interest thereon as it becomes due, as though they were executed by the city of Galesburg, and under her corporate seal."

§ 23. This act shall be attached to the act incorporating the city of Galesburg, and be considered a part of said charter.

§ 24. This act shall not take effect or be in force without a majority of the legal voters of said city shall decide in its favor at an election for that purpose to be held at such time and conducted in such manner as the council of said city may direct.

WM. R. MORRISON,
Speaker of the House of Representatives.

JOHN WOOD,
Speaker of the Senate.

APPROVED, February 18, 1859.

WM. H. BISSELL.

UNITED STATES OF AMERICA, } ss.
STATE OF ILLINOIS.

I, O. M. HATCH, Secretary of State of the State of Illinois, do hereby certify that the foregoing is a true copy of an Enrolled Law, now on file in my office.

{ SEAL. } In witness whereof I have hereunto set my hand and affixed the Great Seal of the State, at the city of Springfield, this 14th day of March, A. D. 1859.

O. M. HATCH,
Secretary of State.

ORDINANCES.

NO. 1.

An Ordinance to define and declare what shall be deemed nuisances in the city of Galesburg, and to authorize and direct the summary abatement thereof, and for the punishment of misdemeanors in said city.

SEC. 1. Be it ordained by the City Council of the city of Galesburg, That the introduction, storing, depositing, or keeping in store or deposit, or on hand, or having in possession within the corporate limits of the city of Galesburg, any spirituous, vinous, malt, fermented, mixed, or intoxicating liquors, for the purpose of bartering, selling or exchanging the same, or for any species of traffic therein, except as hereinafter provided, is hereby declared a public nuisance, and every person guilty thereof, and each and every person knowingly aiding or assisting therein, as agent, clerk, servant or otherwise, shall, upon conviction thereof, forfeit and pay to said city not less than twenty nor more than one hundred dollars.

In every case of conviction under this section it shall be the duty of the court or magistrate rendering judgment, to make it a part of the judgment, that all or any spirituous, vinous, malt, fermented, mixed, or intoxicating liquors found on or about the house or premises of the person or persons, found guilty as aforesaid, for the bartering, selling, or exchanging as aforesaid, shall be taken and destroyed by the City Marshal or other proper officer; said court or magistrate shall issue to the Marshal or other officer, his precept and execution for that purpose, and if any of said liquors are taken away or concealed, the officers may pursue and take the same anywhere within the city.

§ 2. Any person who shall hereafter bring or cause to be brought into this city for sale, or shall sell or offer to sell or keep for sale, any pack of playing cards, dice, billiard table, billiard balls, or any obscene book, pamphlet, or print, shall be deemed guilty of a nuisance, and every such person upon conviction thereof shall be fined any sum not less than ten nor more than one hundred dollars.

In every case of conviction under this section, it shall be the duty of the court or magistrate rendering judgment, to make it a part of the judgment, that any pack of playing cards, dice, billiard table, billiard balls, or any obscene book, pamphlet, or print found on or about the house or premises of the person or persons found guilty as aforesaid, for the purpose of sale or playing, shall be taken and destroyed by the City Marshal or other officer, and the court or magistrate shall issue his precept and execution for that purpose, and if any of said cards, dice, table, balls, book, pamphlet or print, are taken away or concealed, the officer may pursue and take the same anywhere within the city.

§ 3. If any person shall keep, have, or maintain or exercise, a gaming house, table, or room, or in any house or place occupied by him or her, procure or permit any person to frequent, or persons to come together to play for money or valuable thing at any game, and every person knowingly aiding or assisting therein as agent, clerk, servant, or otherwise, such person so offending shall be deemed guilty of a nuisance, and upon conviction thereof shall be fined any sum not less than fifty nor more than one hundred dollars.

In every case of conviction under this section, it shall be the duty of the court or magistrate rendering judgment, to make it a part of the judgment, that any gaming table or other instrument for playing at any game for money or other valuable thing, found on or about the house or premises of the person or persons so found guilty shall be taken and destroyed by the City Marshal or other proper officer, and the court or magistrate shall issue his precept and execution for that purpose, and if such gaming table or gaming instrument be taken away or concealed, the officer may pursue and take the same anywhere within the city.

§ 4. If any person shall be guilty of open lewdness or other notorious act of public indecency, tending to debauch the public morals, or shall keep any tippiing houses, or maintain or keep, or permit in his or her house, a lewd house or place for the practice of fornication, or shall keep a common ill governed or disorderlv house to the encouragement of idleness, drinking, gaming, fornication or other misbehavior, he or she shall be deemed guilty of a nuisance, and upon conviction thereof, shall be fined in any sum not less than twenty nor more than one hundred dollars.

In every case of conviction under this section, the court or magistrate may in their discretion, in rendering judgment, make it a part thereof, that the tippling house, lewd house, or place for the practice of fornication, or any common ill-governed and disorderly house for the encouragement of idleness, drinking, gaming, fornication, or other misbehavior, kept by the person or persons so offending, shall be abated and torn down by the City Marshal or other proper officer, and the court or magistrate may issue his precept and execution for that purpose.

§ 5. Any person who shall sell, barter, or exchange any spirituous, vinous, malt, fermented, mixed, or intoxicating liquors, within the corporation limits of said city, except as hereafter provided, and each and every person knowingly aiding or assisting therein as agent, servant, clerk, or otherwise, shall be adjudged guilty of a nuisance, and upon conviction thereof, shall be fined not less than twenty nor more than one hundred dollars, for each and every offence.

§ 6. Whenever any person shall complain on oath, before any Police Magistrate or Justice of the Peace, that he has good reason to believe and does verily believe, that any vinous, malt, fermented, mixed or intoxicating liquors, are stored or deposited, or held or kept in store on deposit, or on hand, in any store, warehouse, dwelling, room, building, cellar, or other place whatsoever, within the corporate limits of said city, for the purpose of bartering, selling, or exchanging the same, or any species of traffic therein, except as hereinafter provided, or for the purpose of furnishing and delivering the same, for any of the purposes aforesaid, or other purposes in violation of this ordinance, it shall be the duty of said magistrate or justice, to issue a warrant under his hand, directed to the City Marshal, or any constable of said city, reciting the substance of said complaint, and commanding him to forthwith examine the place mentioned in said complaint, and take into his possession all said liquors, found or kept for the purposes aforesaid, which process the Marshal or Constable shall execute, and return with his indorsement showing how he has executed the same. If upon such examination he shall find any of the liquors aforesaid, kept for the purposes aforesaid, he shall take possession thereof, and make his returns aocordingly, stating the name or names of the owner or owners thereof, and the person in whose possession, or charge, or care, the same were found, and thereupon such suits and prosecentions may be instituted as provided in sections one and five of this ordinance, and the marshal or constable in whose possession said liquor may be, shall hold the same in safety, subject to the order and judgment of the magistrate or Justice trying such suit or prosecution.

§ 7. It shall be unlawful to be intoxicated in said city, and any person who shall be found intoxicated therein shall be fined any sum not exceeding ten dollars—Provided, if the liquor upon which such person became intoxicated was procured within the city, in violation of this ordinance, and he will, upon becoming sober, prove from whom it was so procured, he shall be discharged from the fine upon the payment of the costs, and any proper officer, with or without warrant, may arrest any intoxicated person within said city and commit him to the city prison, until he becomes sober, and then convey him before the Magistrate or Justice.

§ 8. The City Council may license any druggist or other person in said city, to keep and sell vinous or alcoholic liquors for sacramental, mechanical, or medicinal purposes, but for no other use or purpose whatsoever.

Any druggist or other person desiring license as aforesaid,

may make application to the council, who shall fix the amount to be paid for the same, and the time said license may run, according to their discretion, and they may require such applicant to give bond and security against the violation of any of the terms of this ordinance, and if such person licensed as aforesaid, shall sell, barter, or exchange, any vinous, spirituous, malt, fermented, mixed, or intoxicating liquors, contrary to his license, or the terms of this ordinance, he shall, upon conviction, be liable to any or all the penalties fixed by this ordinance, and his license shall thereby be revoked and void.

§ 9. If any person or persons shall play for money or other valuable thing, at any game with cards, dice, checks, or at billiards, or with any other article or instrument, thing or things, whatsoever, which may be used for the purpose of playing or betting upon, or winning or losing money, or any other thing or things, article or articles of value, or shall bet on any game others may be playing, within said city, any person so offending shall be fined not less than ten nor more than one hundred dollars.

§ 10. It shall be unlawful to suffer or permit cows, or other neat cattle, horses, hogs, or sheep, to congregate and stay in a body, in any of the public streets or alleys of the city, or to keep or feed them in a body in the streets or alleys, and any person guilty thereof shall be adjudged guilty of a nuisance, and fined not exceeding twenty dollars.

§ 11. Every person who shall be guilty of any assault, assault and battery, affray, riot, rout, unlawful assembly, or disturbing any congregation for religious worship, or who shall willfully disturb the peace or quiet of any neighborhood, family, meeting, congregation, assembly, body of people, or school, by loud or unusual noises, or by tumultuous or offensive carriage, threatening, traducing, quarreling, challenging to fight, or fighting within the limits of said city, shall, upon conviction of either or any of said offenses, be fined in any sum not more than one hundred dollars.

§ 12. Prosecutions for the violation of any of the provisions of this ordinance, except under section six, may be commenced by complaint in writing made and signed by the Mayor, Marshal or City Attorney, without oath, upon which complaint the first process shall be a warrant, and upon complaint by any other person in which case the first process shall be a summons, unless oath or affirmation be made, when a warrant shall issue as in other cases; in either case requiring the person charged te be brought or appear forthwith, and any person or persons, upon whom any fine or penalty is imposed, shall stand committed until the payment of the fine and costs, and in default thereof he may be required to labor on the streets or other public works of said city, under the control and direction of the Street Commissioner, one day for each one dollar of said fine and costs, all of which shall be entered on the docket of the court or magistrate rendering the judgment, the city to furnish him with food and lodging in the city prison or otherwise, during said time. He shall be in the custody of the City Marshal or Street Commissioner, either of whom are hereby required to take charge of and provide for such person, and they are hereby authorized and required to employ all necessary and legal means to prevent his escape, and to retake him when escaped.

§ 13. The Mayor and Aldermen, Marshal, Street Commissioner, Constable and police officers of said city, shall arrest and cause to be arrested, with or without process, all persons who shall break the peace, or threaten to break the peace, or be found violating any ordinance of the city, commit them for examination, and if necessary detain such person in custody over night or the Sabbath day in the watch-house, city prison, or other safe place, or until they can be brought before a magistrate, and it shall be their especial duty to see that the ordinances and laws of the city are complied with, and all offenders brought to justice. All ordinances or parts of ordinances of the town of Galesburg in conflict with this ordinance be and the same are hereby repealed.

PASSED, May 11, 1857.

NO. 2.

An Ordinance additional to an Ordinance entitled an ordinance "to define and declare what shall be deemed nuisances in the City of Galesburg, and to authorize and direct the summary abatement thereof, and for the punishment of misdemeanor in said City," passed May 11, 1857.

§ 1. Be it ordained by the city council of the city of Gales-

burg, That in case of conviction under the fourth section of said ordinance, when the person or persons so convicted are occupying as tenants and not as owners thereof, the tippling house, or place for the practice of fornication, or lewd house, or the common ill-governed and disorderly house, for the keeping of which or either of them the said conviction is obtained, then and in such case the court or magistrate may in their discretion, in rendering judgment make it a part thereof that the person so convicted with all the furniture and household utensils in said house, be removed from said house, and the premises thereof be given to the owner or owners thereof, or his or their agent, and the court or magistrate may issue their precept to the Marshal of the city or other proper officer for that purpose.

PASSED, Aug. 24, 1857.

NO. 3.

An Ordinance to prevent the selling of Liquor to prisoners in the City of Galesburg.

§ 1. Be it ordained by the city council of the city of Galesburg, That it shall be unlawful for any person or persons to furnish intoxicating liquors of any kind, either by sale or otherwise, to any person confined in the city prison.

§ 2. Any person violating this ordinance shall be fined in any sum not exceeding one hundred dollars.

PASSED, October 5, 1857.

NO. 4.

An Ordinance in addition to an Ordinance to define and declare what shall be deemed nuisances in the city of Galesburg, &c., passed May 11, 1857.

§ 1. Be it ordained by the city council of the city of Galesburg, That it shall be unlawful to give away any spirituous, vinous, malt, fermented, mixed or intoxicating liquors, in any saloon, restaurant, eating house, ordinary or other public place within the limits of the city of Galesburg. And each and every person guilty thereof, or knowingly aiding or assisting therein as agent, clerk, servant or otherwise, shall upon conviction thereof, be fined not less than twenty nor more than one hundred dollars.

PASSED, Nov. 30, 1857.

NO. 5.

An Ordinance for the improvement of Streets and and Alleys in the city of Galesburg.

SEC. 1. Grades to be established.
2. Width of side walks; shade trees, how planted.
3. Certain streets to be planked, width thereof, and how same made.
4. Council may excuse portions, and assist in certain cases.
5. Certain walks already made may stand.
6. Improvements not made within thirty days, street commissioner shall make. Commissioner shall make returns to council. Council may make order for collection.
7. Improvements, how made, on petition of owners of two-thirds of property.
8. City shall make crossings and gutters.
9. Streets and sidewalks shall not be obstructed with boxes, rubbish, &c.; punishment for same. Commissioner shall cause same to be done.
10. Sidewalks broken or out of order, Commissioner shall cause same to be repaired. Duty of officers in executing ordinance.

§ 1. Be it ordained by the city council of the city of Galesburg, That the City Surveyor and Engineer be and he is hereby required, under the direction of the committee on streets and improvements, to determine by survey, suitable grades for the streets and alleys of the city, and that the same be done as early as practicable, on the sections of streets hereinafter named, beginning with Main street, and as the same is done, the grade shall be reported to the city council, and if approved by them, shall be the valid and established grade.

§ 2. The sidewalks in said city shall be eight feed wide, except on Main and Broad streets, from North to South streets, and around the Public Square, which shall be 12 feet wide, and on Boon's Avenue, which shall be five feet wide. Wherever there is a continuous line of shade trees now set out in any of the streets, in the future shading of the same the trees shall be set out in the same line, if it can be done without interfering with the use of sidewalks or street, and all trees, posts, or railings, shall be placed on the outer line of the sidewalks.

§ 3. Within thirty days after the establishment of any of the grades as aforesaid, and publication thereof three consecutive days in the daily newspaper, the respective owners of the ground fronting on each established grade, or any of the following sections of streets in said city, namely, on Ferris, Main, Simmons, Tompkins, and South street and around the public square, and on Seminary, Kellogg, Prairie, Cherry, Broad, Cedar and West streets, and Boon's Avenue and Central street, shall, without petition to or further order by the council, make a good and substantial plank sidewalk in front of the ground owned by each as follows: On Main street from Cedar to Prairie streets, it shall be planked twelve feet wide on both sides of the street, the plank not less than two inches thick, laid on four joists six inches wide, and two inches thick, the joists placed on bearers, not more than two feet apart. From Cedar to Academy streets, and from Prairie to Chambers streets, the plank shall be eight feet wide, laid on both sides of the street, and from Chambers street to a point opposite the intersection of the Knoxville road, six feet wide, on the North side of the street only. The sidewalks around the public square shall be planked twelve feet wide, and with plank not less than two inches thick. On Broad street, from the square to South street, the sidewalks shall be planked eight feet wide, and from the square to North street the same width on both sides. On Prairie street from Waters to Brooks street, six feet wide on both sides.

On Cherry street from Waters to Knox street, six feet wide on both sides, except on the west side thereof, opposite the College square, which need not be planked.

On Cedar street, from North to Tompkins street, six feet wide on both sides, and from Tompkins to South street, six feet wide on both sides.

On Kellogg street, from Waters to South street, six feet wide on both sides.

On Seminary street, from North to South, six feet wide on both sides.

On West street, from Main to South, six feet wide on both sides.

On Ferris and Simmons streets, from Seminary to West street, six feet wide on both sides.

On Tompkins and South streets, from Seminary to Academy street, except on the south side of Tompkins street, and the north side of South street, opposite the College square, which need not be planked, six feet wide on both sides.

And on the whole of Boon's Avenue, five feet wide; and Central street, six feet wide on the north side.

In all cases the plank shall be laid on joists two by six inches, not more than two feet apart, supported by bearers not more than two feet apart, and all of the lumber or timber shall be oak, pine or locust. The plank shall in all cases be laid crosswise, and where not otherwise specified, not less than one and a fourth inches thick. Where the whole surface is not planked, one foot shall be left between the ends of the plank and the inside line of the sidewalk. The respective owners shall cut down or fill up, as may be necessary, the ground for the sidewalk in front of their own premises, to the grade established, as aforesaid, and the whole of said improvements shall be made under the direction and control of the street commissioner.

SEC. 4. When there are special and satisfactory reasons to the council, why certain portions of the foregoing improvements should not be made, they may excuse the making thereof, upon application of the owner of the premises, and the council may make provision for filling up, or excavating in certain cases at the expense of the city.

SEC. 5. In all cases where in the opinion of the street commissioner there are good and sufficient sidewalks already made, although they be not as specified in this ordinance, they may continue as though they were in compliance herewith, but when it is necessary to renew the same, they shall be done according to the directions hereof.

§ 6. In case such improvements or any part thereof are not made by the owners of the premises within thirty days after the establishment of the grade and publication thereof, as aforesaid, or the making thereof excuse as aforesaid, it shall be the duty of the street commissioner to cause the same to be made as soon thereafter as practicable, and return to the council all the expense and damage thereof, and the proper amount chargeable to each owner, adding to the amount of each delinquent ten per centum on the cost thereof, for his services, with a specific description of the property, and number of front feet owned by each, and whether the owners be residents or non residents, minors or married women, and all other facts relative thereto. The council may thereupon determine whether they will bring suit against the owners of the premises, for what each ought to pay, or they may assess and collect the same from the property owned by each fronting the improvement, in their discretion, with interest from the date of the return made by the commissioner, and cost, by an order to be entered in their proceedings upon the lots or lands respectively, and collect the same by warrant and sale of the premises as in other cases.

§ 7. Whenever the owners of two-thirds of the property fronting on other portions of said streets or on any other street or alley of the city, or section thereof, shall, by petition to the council showing the number of front feet owned by each, ask to have said street or the sidewalks thereof, or any section thereof graded, regraded, leveled, paved, planked, shaded, guttered, drained or otherwise improved, the council may pass an order requiring the same to be done at such time and in such manner as they may think proper, and assess the expense and damage thereof upon all the property fronting on the portion of street to be improved equally per front foot, or assess upon each owner or the property of each owner the amount of the expense and damages occasioned by the improvement in front of his or her specific property, or they mav assess different portions of said property at different rates as the same shall be just and equitable, and they may collect the amount which each owner ought to pay by suit, or off some by suit, and others by assessment and sale of the pemises as aforesaid or so much as may be necessary.

§ 8. In all cases contemplated by this ordinance where an order is made by the council for making any improvement, they shall provide for making good and substantial crossings or gutters, when necessary, at the expense of the city, over every street crossed by the improvement.

§ 9. It shall be unlawful for any person to put any obstruction, boxes, ashes, offal or rubbish, whatever, upon or into any street, sidewalk, lane, alley, public square or gutter of said city, and upon conviction thereof, any person so offending shall be fined not exceeding ten dollars—and it shall be the duty of the occupant of the premises fronting on any sidewalk, or gutter, to keep the same clear of snow, ice, manure, or other offal or rubbish, and upon failure to do so, the Street Commissioner shall cause the same to be done at the expense of such occupant, for which he shall be liable upon suit in the name of the city. Provided, however, that this section shall not apply to cases of removal, receiving or sending away goods, where not more than one-third of the sidewalk is occupied, nor shall it apply to the use and occupation of one third of the sidewalk on the side next the building, for the purpose of showing and exhibiting goods, wares, or merchandise.

§ 10. In all cases when the sidewalks of the city get out of repair, the planks broken, or otherwise, it shall be the duty of the Street Commissioner to have the same repaired immediately, at the expense of the owner of the property, and if the amount thereof be not paid by the owner on demand, he shall bring suit therefor in the name of the city, or may return same to the council who may order it to be assessed and collected by the sale of the premises as in other cases.

It shall be the especial duty of the City Marshal and Street Commissioner to see that this ordinance is observed and carried into faithful execution, and all ordinances of the town of Galesburg, conflicting with this ordinance are hereby repealed.

PASSED, May 11, 1857.

NO. 6.

An Ordinance to amend the Ordinance for the improvement of Streets and Alleys, passed May 11, 1857.

§ 1. Be it ordained by the city council of the city of Galesburg, That said ordinance be and the same is hereby so amended, That it shall be the duty of the respective owners of the ground fronting on any of the portions of the streets in said ordinance named, at any time after ten days notice by the Street Commissioner, whether the grade of the street be established or not, to plank the sidewalks in front of such ground, in the way and manner as in said ordinance is provided, under the direction and control of the Street Commissioner. So much of said ordinance as requires the grades of any of the streets, to be established by the Council, and publication thereof made, before the owners of the ground fronting thereon, are required to plank the sidewalks, be and the same is hereby repealed.

PASSED, June 5, 1857.

NO. 7.

An Ordinance prescribing the duties of the Board of Health, and affixing penalties for disobedience to their orders.

§ 1. Be it ordained by the city council of the city of Galesburg, That it shall be the duty of the Board of Health of said city to take all necessary and immediate steps to prevent the spread or introduction of dangerous disease. They shall have power for that purpose to prevent or disperse meetings of individuals within an infected district. They may enter all houses or other places, public or private, at all times when necessary, in the exercise of said powers, and in so doing, may exercise all the powers of Marshal or Street Commissioner, or call to their aid the services of said officers, when in their judgment circumstances require it. And any person failing or refusing to observe the orders and regulations of the Board, shall, upon conviction, be subject to imprisonment in the city prison, not exceeding thirty days, and to pay the costs of prosecution.

It is hereby declared by the unanimous vote of the council, that an emergency exists sufficient to dispense with the publication of this ordinance, and it shall take effect and be in force immediately after its passage.

PASSED, May 29, 1857.

NO. 8.

An Ordinance to provide for Licenses in the City of Galesburg.

§ 1. Be it ordained by the city council of the city of Galesburg, That it shall be unlawful for any person to exercise within the limits of this city, the business of a merchandise or real estate broker, the business of insurance, including agencies and home companies, pawn-broker, the business of a hawker, peddler, auctioneer, livery stable keepers, storage, forwarding, or commission merchant, confectioner, or to keep any ice cream saloon, eating house, restaurant, ordinary, inn, or tavern, or meat market, or to sell fresh meat in the streets in less quantities than a quarter, or to exhibit any circus, equestrian exhibition, menagerie, musical party, concert, theatrical performance, exhibition of rope or wire dancing, puppets, wax figures, paintings, statuary, tricks of legerdemain, or any other exhibition, show or amusement, or to run any hackney carriage, omnibus, cab, cabriolet, cart, wagon, dray or other vehicle used for conveying persons, for hire, without license therefor: Provided, That the provisions of this section shall not apply to musical parties, concerts, or thespian performances for benevolent or charitable purposes, or exhibitions of any literary or scientific institution or school situated within this city, or when the company is composed or controlled by residents of this city.

§ 2. A merchandise broker is one, who for a commission or other compensation, is engaged in selling, or who negotiates sales of goods, wares, or merchandise, belonging to others.

§ 3. A real estate broker is one who for a commission or other compensation, is engaged in selling, or who negotiates sales of real estate belonging to others.

§ 4. Any person who loans money on deposit of personal property, or who deals in the purchasing of personal property on condition of selling the same back again at a stipulated price, is declared to be a pawn-broker.

§ 5. A keeper of an ordinary is one who sells, or offers for sale in any house, cellar, or booth, shed or stand, any article of meat, fruit, or other food to be used, eaten, or consumed in or at the place of sale.

§ 6. There shall be levied and collected on every license granted for any business or object herein specified, such sum, in cash, as the city council shall by resolution of record from time to time declare. Save only that upon a license for an exhibition of a circus, equestrian exhibition, or menagerie, not less than ten nor more than one hundred dollars per day, to be fixed at the discretion of the Mayor.

Upon a license for a musical party, concert, theatrical performance, exhibition of rope or wire dancing, puppets, wax figures, paintings, statuary, tricks of legerdemain, or other exhibition or performance within the meaning of this ordinance, not less than five nor more than fifty dollars for the first day, and not less than three nor more than twenty-five dollars for each subsequent day, at the discretion of the Mayor.

§ 7. All licenses issued under the provisions of this ordinance, shall bear date the day of their issue and expire the fifteenth day of April following, except those provided for in section six of this ordinance, and where the council in special cases shall order otherwise.

§ 8. All licenses granted in pursuance of the provisions of this ordinance, shall be subject to the ordinances of the city existing when they are issued or subsequently passed.

§ 9. All licenses shall be issued by the city clerk under the seal of the city, and be signed by the Mayor and countersigned by the clerk, and state the name of the person licensed, the nature of the business to be licensed, the date of granting the same, and how long it is to continue in force.

§ 10. No license shall be granted by the city clerk until the person asking the license shall have deposited with the clerk the receipt of the city treasurer acknowledging the receipt, in cash, of the amount required to be paid for such license, which receipt shall be preserved by the Clerk. The violation of this section by the clerk shall render him personally liable to the city for said amount in cash.

§ 11. Any person desiring a license under the provisions of this ordinance, shall apply to the city treasurer, and upon payment to said treasurer of the full amount required for the license, in cash, the treasurer shall give him a receipt therefor expressing the amount as paid, in cash, and the kind of license required, and upon presentment of said receipt to the Clerk, the applicant shall be entitled to a license upon paying the clerk fifty cents for issuing the same. But the receipt of the treasurer shall not authorize the holder thereof to exercise the business for which a license is required, and any person carrying on such business upon such receipt without a license, shall be liable to the penalties which are provided against those who carry on without a license any business or calling requiring a license under this ordinance.

§ 12. Every person holding a license from the city, shall be required to show the same to the City Marshal at any time upon demand therefor; any person neglecting or refusing to do so shall be liable to the penalties provided by this ordinance against persons carrying on the business or occupation herein mentioned, without a license.

§ 13. No license granted by this city shall be assignable or transferrable, nor shall any such license authorize any person to do business or act under it but the person named therein, or at more than one place, if the business is local.

§ 14. Whoever shall violate, or neglect, or refuse to conform to and observe the provisions of this ordinance, shall, upon conviction thereof, be fined not less than ten nor more than one hundred dollars, and in case the offender has no license he shall also be liable to the city for the amount required for such license, to be recovered in an action brought in the name of the city, against such offender.

§ 15. It shall be the duty of the city clerk to keep a list of all the persons who shall have taken out a license from the city, which list shall contain the name of the grantee, the the business licensed, the amount paid, the date and duration of the license; the neglect of this duty shall render the

Clerk liable to the fine spcified in the next preceding section.

§ 16. It shall be the duty of the Marshal to inform the Mayor of every infraction of this ordinance, and for every conviction for any violation of this ordinance, the Marshal shall receive the sum of one dollar in addition to his regular fees, to be paid when the fine is collected.

§ 17. All drays, wagons and carts running or being run for hire within the corporate limits of said city shall be subject to the following restrictions and regulations:

First, It shall be the duty of every person wishing to run any dray, wagon, or cart, to pay over to the city treasurer before proceeding to run the same, the sum of five dollars for each dray or wagon, and the sum of two dollars and fifty cents for each cart being or intended to be run in said city for hire.

Second, It shall be the further duty of every such person running any dray, wagon, or cart as aforesaid, or intending to do so, to procure a number for the same from the city clerk, and place the same in some conspicuous place on such dray, wagon, or cart, and to have the same renewed annually.

Third, It shall be the duty of every person running any dray, wagon or cart as aforesaid, when demanded of him, to convey or transport any goods, wares, merchandise, or any article whatever, to any part of the corporate limits of the city. And such person may charge for every dray load, twenty-five cents for the distance of three-fourths of a mile and under, and no more. For a wagon load for the same distance, thirty cents; between that distance and one mile, for a dray load, forty cents; over one mile, fity cents. And for either of the said last named distances, for a wagon load, fifty cents. Every person disobeying the provisions of this section, shall be fined not less than three nor more than twenty dollars and costs.

§ 18. All fines, penalties, or forfeitures accruing under this ordinance regulating the running of drays, wagons and carts, for hire, shall be a lien on the carriage run by any persons without a license, and the Marshal may seize the same at the time of serving process upon the offender, or at any time after, and keep the same until the final determination of the case, and if such suit shall finally terminate against the defendant, the Marshal shall proceed to sell such carriage immediately, unless all fines and costs growing out of such suit shall be forthwith paid over to said city; the proceeds of such sale to be appropriated toward paying the fine and costs; the overplus, if any, to be paid over to the other party.

§ 19. That any person or persons, who shall knowingly sell any flesh of any diseased animal, or other unwholesome provisions, shall be fined not less than ten nor more than one hundred dollars.

§ 20. All persons convicted of a violation of any of the provisions of this ordinance shall stand committed until the fine and costs are paid, and upon the failure to pay the same, he may be required to labor on the streets or other public works of the city, one day for each dollar of the fine and costs, and the city shall furnish him with food and lodging in the city prison until the same be discharged.

§ 21. That the Mayor may, when good cause is shown, and he is empowered to do so, cancel and revoke any license granted under the provisions of this ordinance, and he is hereby authorized in his discretion to fix the amount to be paid for a hawker's or peddlar's license, from one to five dollars per day.

PASSED, June 5, 1857.

NO. 9.

An ordinance fixing the amount to be paid for licenses in the city of Galesburg.

§ 1. Be it ordained by the city council of the city of Galesburg, That every merchandise broker shall pay for license to carry on his business in the city of Galesburg, from five to twenty five dollars, in the discretion of the Mayor.

Every Real Estate broker, twenty-five dollars.

Every pawn-broker, fifty dollars.

Every keeper of an Ordinary, five dollars.

Every person engaged in the business of Insurance, including agencies or home companies, ten dollars; and where the same person is agent for, or represents more companies than one, he shall pay the same amount for a license for each company or agency.

Every Auctioneer, from twenty-five to one hundred dollars, in the discretion of the Mayor.

Every Livery Stable keeper, ten dollars.

Every Storage, Forwarding, or Commission merchant, ten dollars.

Every Confectioner, five dollars.

Every keeper of an Ice Cream Saloon, ten dollars.

Every keeper of an Eating House, ten dollars.

Every keeper of a Restaurant, ten dollars.

Every keeper of an Inn or Tavern, from twenty-five to fifty dollars, in the discretion or the Mayor.

Every keeper of a Meat Market, twenty five dollars.

Every person who sells fresh meat in the street, in less quantity than a quarter, ten dollars; provided, however, that nothing herein contained shall prevent a licensed keeper of a meat market from sending or selling meat in his wagon to or in any part of the city.

Every one who runs a hackney coach, carriage, omnibus, cab, cabriolet, or other vehicle used for conveying persons or property for hire, except drays, wagons, or carts, ten dollars; provided, however, that a firm composed of more than one, doing business together in good faith, may do so, under the same license; and the business of a confectioner, keeper of an ice cream saloon, eating house, restaurant and ordinary, or any one or more of them, may be done under the same license, paying for the same not less than ten dollars, but not in more than one place in said city.

PASSED, June 22, 1857.

NO. 10.

An ordinance to amend the ordinance passed June 22, 1857, fixing the amount to be paid for licenses.

§ 1. Be it ordained by the city council of the city of Galesburg, That every keeper of an Inn or Tavern, shall pay for license, not less than ten, nor more than fifty dollars, in the discretion of the Mayor. Which license shall also confer upon the proprietor of the Inn or Tavern the privilege of running an omnibus for the same, free of charge.

PASSED, Aug. 24, 1857.

[This ordinance is modified so as to permit the Mayor to charge amount according to time the license has to run.]

NO. 11.

Requiring Barber Shops in the city of Galesburg to be closed on the Sabbath day.

§ 1. Be it ordained by the city council of the city of Galesburg, That it shall be unlawful to open, or keep open, for the purpose of business, any barber shop within the limits of said city, on Sunday; and every person so transgressing shall be fined from one to ten dollars for each offense.

PASSED, June 15, 1857.

NO. 12.

An ordinance regulating the building of Privies, and requiring Livery and Public Stables to be cleansed.

§ 1. Be it ordained by the city council of the city of Galesburg, That it shall be the duty of each and every person hereafter building a privy in said city to provide the same with a vault at least five feet deep, and sufficiently walled up; also, to provide the same with a good and sufficient ventilator.

§ 2. It shall be the duty of every person owning a privy in said city, to deposit in the vault of the same, half a bushel of unslacked lime in each of the following months, to-wit: June, July, August and September in every year.

§ 3. It shall be the duty of each and every owner of any livery or public stable within said city, to remove all dung, manure or trash, once in every week from their premises, from the first of April to the first of November in every year.

§ 4. Every person neglecting or refusing to comply with the foregoing provisions of this ordinance, shall forfeit and pay a fine of not more than twenty-five dollars.

PASSED, June 15, 1857.

NO. 13.

An Ordinance relating to dogs running at large in the city of Galesburg.

§ 1. Be it ordained by the city council of the city of Galesburg, That no dog or slut kept within the limits of said city, shall run at large within said limits, unless the owner thereof shall put upon such dog or slut, a collar made of metal or a collar having a metal plate on which the name of such owner shall be inscribed in plain letters, and unless such owner shall give his name and a description of such dog or slut to the city clerk, who shall register the same in a book kept for that purpose, and at the same time pay the cityTreasurer a tax of one dollar for each dog and five dollars for each slut kept by him and suffered to run at large, and thereafter annually pay a like tax on such dog or slut. He shall also pay said clerk twenty-five cents for making said registry.

§ 2. Be it further ordained, That every dog or slut running at large contrary to the provisions of this ordinance, shall be deemed a nuisance, and the owner thereof shall forfeit and pay for the use of said city, the sum of five dollars.

§ 3. Be it further ordained, That every dog or slut running at large contrary to the provisions of this ordinance, shall be killed by or under the direction of the City Marshal, for which he shall be paid out of the city treasury fifty cents for each dog or slut so killed.

§ 4. That no person shall in any way attempt to prevent, or prevent the Marshal or any person acting under his direction from performing any duty required by this ordinance, and any person so offending shall forfeit and pay for the use of said city not less than five nor more than twenty dollars.

§ 5. This ordinance shall not apply to any dog or slut under the age of two months, or that may be brought into the city by its owner, such owner not being a resident, until such dog or slut shall have been in the city three days.

§ 6. The Mayor may from time to time, on an alarm of "mad dogs," in his discretion prohibit by notice in a public newspaper, all dogs from running at large within the limits of the city, and may appoint deputies with authority to kill all dogs or sluts running at large within the city, and such prohibition may continue so long as the public safety, in the opinion of the Mayor may require, and such prohibition shall remain in force until the Mayor shall give public notice of the discontinuance thereof.

PASSED, June 29, 1857.

NO. 14.

An ordinance in reference to resisting officers in the city.

§ 1. Be it ordained by the City Council of the city of Galesburg, That any person who shall hinder, obstruct, resist or otherwise interfere with any city or other officer in the city of Galesburg, in the discharge of his official duties, or attempt to prevent any such officer from arresting any person in his custody, shall be deemed guilty of a misdemeanor.

§ 2. Whoever shall be convicted of a misdemeanor, under the provisions of this ordinance, shall be fined not less than five nor more than one hundred dollars; and the person so fined shall be imprisoned in the Calaboose until the fine and costs are paid; and it shall be the duty of the court or magistrate before whom such offender is convicted, to enter as a part of the judgment, that the person so fined shall be committed to the calaboose until the fine and costs shall be paid.

PASSED, July 3, 1857

NO. 15.

An Ordinance relating to animals running at large in the City of Galesburg.

§ 1. Be it ordained by the city council of the city of Galesburg, That it shall be unlawful for horses, cattle, asses, mules or sheep, to run at large within the city of Galesburg, between one hour after sunset and sunrise, and the owner thereof suffering or permitining it, shall be subject to a fine in the name of the city of not less than one or more than ten dollars for each and every animal so running at large.

§ 2. If any animal shall at any time break into, through, or over any fence or enclosure in said city, three feet high, or be caught in the act of breaking into, through, or over any such fence or enclosure, it shall be lawful for the owner or occupier of such fence or enclosure, or of the lot or premises on which it stands, to seize and take up such animal, and secure and detain it, in a sufficient barn, lot, or enclosure, or by fastening it with a rope or other fastening, and he shall thereupon, within twelve hours, deliver to the clerk of said city, a short description of such animals, stating when and where and by whom it was taken up, which the clerk shall note down in a book kept for that purpose, and he shall post a notice thereof upon a board to be kept at the street entrance to the office of the city council.

§ 3. It shall be the duty of such taker up, to keep such animal secured as aforesaid, and to supply it with sufficient and reasonable food and water, and if it be a horse, mule, or ass, he shall keep it ten days, or if it be a bull, steer, cow, calf or sheep, he shall keep it five days, and at any time thereafter, without further notice, he may put such animal up at public auction, and sell the same on the public square in said city, to the highest and best bidder for cash in hand, and the purchaser shall hold and own the animal sold as aforesaid, absolutely without any right of redemption.

§ 4. The taker up of such animal shall be allowed for keeping same as long as he may see proper to do so, not less than ten and five days, as aforesaid, fifty cents per day, if a horse, mule or ass, and twenty five cents per day for every other animal herein mentioned, The party injured shall be paid for all injury or damage sustained by reason of such animal breaking or attempting to break into, through, or over his fence or premises as aforesaid, and if it is not known by the taker up, by which one the fence was broken down, then the damages shall be equally assessed on all of them: but if it be known by which animal or animals the fence or enclosure was broken, then the damages shall be charged upon them up to their value, and the ballance assessed equally upon the remaining animals; and all the costs, keeping and damages herein provided for, shall be paid out of the proceeds of such sale, and the balance, if any, paid to the owner of the animal or animals sold as aforesaid, if it be demanded; otherwise it shall be delivered to the city clerk, with a short return of the sale, of which he shall make an entry, and pay the money into the city treasury, and the same may be drawn from there at any time within three months, but not afterwards.

§ 5. To ascertain the amount of injury or damage sustained, as aforesaid, the taker up of animal or animals shall cause the amount thereof to be assessed by two reputable freeholders of said city, if they can agree; if not, they shall choose a third, all of whom shall be sworn, and their assessment shall be binding and final upon the parties. And in all matters arising under this ordinance, all and any facts may be established by the oath or affidavit of the taker up or injured party, and no further testimony shall be necessary. Provided, however, that nothing in this ordinance contained, shall prevent other witnesses being examined by the referees, and they may examine the premises, nor shall it prevent any fact or thing being inquired into or proved or disproved in a proper action to be brought by any person interested, but in any such action the taker up or the injured person shall always be allowed the benefit of his oath or affidavit.

§ 6. The city clerk is hereby authorized to administer any oath herein required, for which he may charge a fee of twenty five cents, and he shall be paid a fee of twenty five cents each for the duties required under sections two and four of this ordinance.

Passed, July 17, 1857.

NO. 16.

An ordinance to amend the ordinance relating to animals running at large, passed July 17, 1857.

Sec. 1. Be it ordained by the city council of the city of Galesburg, That the ordinance relating to animals running at large, passed July 17, 1857, be, and the same is hereby so amended, That beyond one mile from the centre of Main and Cherry streets of said city, a board fence shall be four feet high and a rail fence four and one-half feet high, before any animal breaking through, or attempting to break through the same, shall be subject to be taken up, as in said ordinance is provided. And the taker up of any animal under said ordinance or this amendment, shall instead of twelve hours, have thirty six hours from the time of taking up the animal to deliver to the city clerk the description thereof, and time and place ot taking up the same; and all animals shall be kept by the taker up ten days, except horses, mules and asses, which shall be kept thirty days, before sale thereof.

§ 2. Be it further ordained, That all sales made of such animals, shall be made by the City Marshal, or a constable, and before making the same, the taker up shall give three days' previous notice, by one publication in a weekly newspaper published in said city.

The officer selling the same shall be allowed one dollar for selling each horse, mule or ass, and fifty cents each for all other animals, and out of the proceeds of the sale he shall first pay all cost, then the expenses and damages sustained from the animal, and the balance to the owner of the animal if demanded, otherwise he shall immediately pay it into the city treasury, from which it may be drawn by the owner at any time within one year from such sale.

§ 3. If any person shall take away or out of the possession of the taker up, without his consent, any animal taken up under said ordinance or this amendment without the payment, or tender of the amount which may be due by reason of such tresspassing animal, he shall be fined any sum not less than double the amount which may be due as aforesaid, out of which shall be paid the costs, expenses, and damages as aforesaid, and the balance into the city treasury.

Passed, August 17, 1857.

NO. 17.

An ordinance relating to hotel and other runners and porters in the City of Galesburg.

SEC. 1. Be it ordained by the City Council of the City of Galesburg, That it shall be unlawful for any hotel to have more than one runner or porter on the ground of any railroad company, whose depot is within the limits of said city, to solicit passengers.

§ 2. Each runner or porter is required to wear a badge bearing the name of the house which he represents.

§ 3. The proprietors of hotels, if engaged in soliciting custom, shall be considered as runners, and subjected to the same rules and penalties.

§ 4. It shall be unlawful for any person to talk in a loud or boisterous manner on the depot grounds, or to call the name of any house with a view to attract the attention of passengers, except at the door of the omnibus, and then not in a boisterous manner.

§ 5. Upon the arrival of a train, no runner or porter shall cross either track, but shall be confined to the outside platform made for the convenience of carriages.

After baggage is ready for delivery, runners or porters holding checks may cross the tracks to claim baggage.

§ 6. No person shall secretly solicit passengers in or about the passenger building.

§ 7. The penalty for the violation of any part of the above ordinance, shall be a fine of not less than one or more than ten dollars, to be recovered by complaint before a Magistrate.

§ 8. A policeman shall be stationed at the depot, whose duty it shall be to enforce this ordinance and to arrest, with or without process, on the spot, any person found violating any of its provisions, who shall not be discharged from custody until payment of the fine and costs; and the Magistrate may, in default thereof, commit him to the calaboose, or to work on the streets or other public works of the city.

PASSED Sept. 28, 1857.

NO. 18.

An ordinance to direct the manner of proceeding in all cases of violation of city ordinances.

SEC. 1. Be it ordained by the City Council of the City of Galesburg, That prosecutions for the violation of any ordinance, or of any provisions of any ordinance, which has been or may be passed by the said City Council, except when otherwise provided in any such ordinance, may be commenced by complaint in writing, made and signed by the Mayor, Marshal or Attorney of said city, without an oath, or by complaint in writing of any other person on oath or affirmation, in either of which cases a warrant shall issue from the Magistrate with whom such complaint is filed, requiring the person or persons charged to be brought forthwith before said magistrate, or any other officer in said city of competent jurisdiction. *Provided*, however, that section thirteenth of an ordinance entitled an ordinance to define and declare what shall be deemed nuisances in the city of Galesburg, and to authorize and direct the summary abatement thereof, and for the punishment of misdemeanors in said city, passed May 11, 1857, or any other section of said ordinance, shall not be repealed by this ordinance.

§ 2. Any person or persons upon whom any fine or penalty is imposed for the breach of any ordinance which has or may be passed by the said city council, shall, in the discretion of the Magistrate, stand committed to the city prison until the payment of the fine and costs, or be required to work on the streets or other public works of said city, under the control or direction of the Street Commissioner, one day for each one dollar of said fine and costs, in either of which cases the Magistrate shall issue process accordingly, the city to furnish the person or persons so working food and lodging in the city prison, or otherwise, during said time. The person or persons so required to work shall be in the custody of the Street Commissioner, who is authorized and required to take charge of and provide for such person or persons, and to employ all necessary and legal means to prevent his or their escape, and to retake him or them in case of escape.

Passed Oct. 5, 1857.

NO. 19.

An ordinance to establish and regulate the police department of the City of Galesburg, and for the punishment of disorderly conduct therein.

Sec. 1. Establishing a police department in the city of Galesburg.
2. Policemen, how appointed and removed.
3. Mayor to haye supervision; his powers and duties.
4. Marshal; his powers and duties.

5. Officers powers and duties in arresting offenders.
6. Persons arrested, when may give bail. Form of.
7. Penalty for official negligence.
8. City Calaboose or jail.
9. Police officers may demand aid in making arrests.
10. Poliee be called out by Mayor, Alderman, or Police Magistrate.
11. Certain offences described. Penalty.
12. Magistrate may take recognizance, or commit.

SEC. 1. Be it ordained by the City Council of the City of Galesburg, That there shall be, and is hereby established in said city, a police department, to consist of the Mayor, Marshal, and such policemen as are now, or may hereafter be appointed.

§ 2. Policemen shall be appointed by the Council or Mayor, shall hold their appointment for the time specified in the order of making their appointment, but may be removed any time by the Mayor, for cause, or by the Council at any time they see proper to do so, without cause; and they shall receive such salary as may be determined by the Council.

§ 3. The Mayor shall have the general supervision and control of the police. He shall from time to time make such regulations touching their duties under the ordinance, as to him shall seem best for the maintenance of order, and for enforcing a due observance of the ordinances of the city. He shall require of the city police a strict performance of their duties; and in case of the neglect or refusal of any policeman to perform his duty, or for drinking intoxicating liquors, or drunken or riotous conduct, it shall be his duty to discharge the policeman so doing, neglecting or refusing, immediately, and appoint a substitute, if necessary.

§ 4. The City Marshal shall be the chief of the city police, subordinate only to the Mayor, or Council when in session, and all policemen shall be subordinate to him only as provided by ordinance. It shall be his duty to collect all dues owing to the city, not within the province of the Treasurer to collect. He shall see that the side walks, streets, alleys, and other avenues of the city are kept free from boxes, rubbish and other impediments, and that all ordinances are strictly observed.

It shall be his duty to see that the policemen are on duty at night, when necessary, appoint their different districts or beats each evening, and in case of sickness or necessary absence of any policeman, employ a substitute until the return of the absentee or meeting of the Council. It shall also be his duty at the first meeting of the Council in each month, to report the number of days and nights each policeman has been on service the previous month, verified by oath.

§ 5. It shall be the duty of all policemen to meet at such place and times as may be designated by the Marshal, and continue in active duty as long as required. All members of the police department, and all constables in said city, shall have power and authority, for the purpose of making arrests and quelling disorders and disturbances, to enter in a peaceable manner, or if resisted after demand is made, with force, into any house, store, shop, grocery or other building whatever, where any illegal practice or violation of any ordinance is being carried on, or where there is probable and reasonable cause for supposing the same is being carried on, and shall, to the best of their ability, preserve order, peace and quiet throughout the city. They shall arrest, with or without warrant, any person found violating any law or ordinance; any person making loud or unusual noises, or otherwise unnecessarily disturbing the quiet and order of the city; any person found at any time, by day or night, in a state of intoxication, in any street, side walk, alley or exposed place in said city; any person who shall, by exhibiting in said city any indecent act or conduct calculated to disturb the peace and good order of the city, by collecting crowds in the streets, sidewalks, or elsewhere in said city; any person using, in any public or exposed place in said city, any obscene, profane, blasphemous or boisterous language; any person who may be found lurking about under suspicious circumstances, and secure them for examination; and the officer making the arrest shall forthwith take the arrested before a police magistrate, to be dealt with according to law and the ordinances of the city. Should such arrest be made in the night time, or when the police court is not in session, he shall convey the party to the city jail or calaboose, and there detain him until the opening of the police court, unless bail is given, as provided in section six of this ordinance. And any of said arrests may be made on the Sabbath day.

§ 6. Any person arrested without warrant in the night time, or the Sabbath, or when the police court is not in session, or otherwise engaged, for any offence, shall have the right to release himself or herself from custody by giving bail to the officer for his or her appearance before the police court at any time, to be named in the recognizance, which shall be as early as practicable, to answer for the offence for which he was arrested; which recognizance shall be as follows in substance:

We, A. B. and C. D., acknowledge ourselves jointly and severally bound unto the city of Galesburg, in the penal sum of one hundred dollars. *Provided*, That if said A. B. shall appear before————Police Magistrate, at — o'clock, on ——day of ————, and pay whatever judgment may be rendered against him for [naming the offence] or render his body in obedience to said judgment, then this obligation to be void.

A. B. [SEAL.]
C. D. [SEAL.]

Said recognizance shall be returned by the officer taking it, and at the time named therein, or any time thereafter, the magistrate may try the cause, whether the person arrested be present or not. If he be not present, and the fine not paid immediately, judgment shall then be rendered against the surety on said recognizance for the amount thereof.—*Provided*, That if the trial be not at the time named in the recognizance, the defendants shall have notice thereof.

§ 7. Any person now holding, or appointed to any office under the provisions of this ordinance, who shall be negligent or careless in the performance of his duties, shall, on conviction, be fined not less than five nor more than fifty dollars, and forfeit all arrears that may be due him from the city for service in said office.

§ 8. There shall be designated by the Council a calaboose, jail, or city prison for the confinement and punishment of such offenders as shall fail or refuse to pay any fines or forfeitures rendered against them, or shall fail or refuse to give bail when arrested to answer for any violation of any ordinance of the city, or shall be subject to imprisonment under any ordinance of the city. The Marshal shall have charge of the calaboose, subject to the control of the Council; and until further order, the frame building in the rear of the engine house shall be the city calaboose.

§ 9. The Mayor, Marshal and every police officer, shall have power to call upon any inhabitant of the city to assist in quelling any riotous or disorderly conduct, or to aid in the arrest and safe keeping of any person accused of crime, or breach of law or ordinance; and any one so called, who shall neglect or refuse to give such aid or assistance, shall be

subject to a fine of not more than fifty dollars, to be recovered as in other cases of breach of the ordinances of said city.

§ 10. The city police shall be subject, at all times, day or night, to be called out by the Mayor, Aldermen or Police Magistrates, to make arrests, quell disorders, maintain peace, or suppress riots in said city.

§ 11. It shall be unlawful within said city, for any person to make loud and unusual noises, or otherwise unnecessarily disturb the peace, quiet and order of the city; for any person, by day or by night, in any street, side walk, public or exposed place in said city, to be found in a state of intoxication; any person to be guilty of any act or exhibition calculated to disturb the peace and good order of the city, by collecting crowds in the streets, side walks or elsewhere; for any person to use, in any public or exposed place, or in crowds, obscene, profane, blasphemous or boisterous language; for any person to be found lurking about under suspicious circumstances.

It shall be unlawful to play at any game, or to be engaged in or about any unnecessary or unbecoming amusement, or labor in said city on the Sabbath day.

It shall be unlawful to keep open on Saturday night any public place, house or business, except public hotels, later than eleven o'clock.

It shall be the duty of every magistrate, or other officer who shall receive any money belonging to the city from fines or otherwise, to pay the same immediately to the treasurer, and at the end of each month every magistrate before whom any judgment shall have been rendered in the name of the city, shall report to the council a full account of fines assessed by him, and against whom assessed, the amount collected and from whom, and for each failure to make such return, he shall be fined not less than five dollars.

And while in default as aforesaid, no prosecution shall be commenced before him in the name of the city.

Every person guilty of any of said offences, or of violating any of the provisions of this ordinance, or neglecting or refusing to obey any of its provisions, shall, upon conviction, be fined not exceeding fifty dollars.

§ 12. In all cases of arrest under any ordinance of the city, the magistrate may permit the party arrested to go on recognizance, with sufficient surety entered and signed on his docket, to such time as may be set for hearing, or may commit to the calaboose, at his discretion.

Passed Oct. 19th, 1857.

NO. 20.

An ordinance to regulate teams, fast riding, and hitching, in the City of Galesburg.

SEC. 1. Be it ordained by the City Council of the City of Galesburg, That it shall be unlawful to leave any horse, or mule, or team of any kind standing in any street, or public place in said city, unless the animal or team is securely fastened or hitched, or is in the care of the owner or driver of the same.

SEC. 2. It shall be unlawful to hitch or fasten any horse, or mule, or other team, to any shade tree growing in any of the streets or public places in said city, or to any boxing placed around the same. Any person convicted of a violation of either of the above sections, shall be fined the sum of one dollar for each and every offence.

SEC. 3. It shall be unlawful to drive upon or across any sidewalk in said city, with any horse, mule, or team of any kind, except at proper crossing places. Any person convicted of a violation of this section, shall be fined a sum not exceeding five dollars.

SEC. 4. It shall be unlawful to ride or drive any horse, mule, or other beast or team, in any street, square, or other public place in said city, faster than a moderate gait, except in case of urgent necessity; or wilfully or carelessly to ride or drive any animal so as to cause it, or any vehicle attached to it, to come in collision with any other object or person.— Any person violating any provision of this section shall, on conviction, be fined a sum not exceeding twenty dollars.

All ordinances of the town of Galesburg coflicting with this ordinance are hereby repealed.

Passed Nov. 23, 1857.

NO. 21.

An ordinance for the regulation and government of the City Prison.

SEC. 1. Be it ordained by the City Council of the City of Galesburg, That the building erected by the city on lots number one and two, on block number eighteen, on the west side of Cedar street, in the city of Galesburg, be and the same is hereby designated as the city calaboose or prison.

SEC. 2. The Marshal of said city shall have the charge and be the keeper of said prison, and with the consent of the Council, and not otherwise, he may appoint a deputy or substitute for the keeping thereof. He shall be responsible for the acts or omissions of his said deputy, as though the act or omission were done by himself. Said deputy or substitute shall also be responsible for his own acts or omissions, as though he were principal. Provided, That nothing in this section or any other ordinance contained, shall prevent the Council from removing any such keeper at pleasure, and appoint another in his stead.

SEC. 3. It shall be the duty of the keeper to receive into said prison all persons committed to the same by any police magistrate, justice of the peace, police officer, watchman or other city officer, who shall be charged with, in custody, or convicted for the violation of any ordinances of the city, or any breach of the peace. He shall keep a register, in which he shall enter the names of all persons committed, the time when, for what time, and for what offence committed, and such other facts as he may deem necessary.

SEC. 4. It shall be the duty of said keeper to receive into said prison, for keeping over night, or other short period, any prisoner in custody of any other officer for any offence against the laws of the State of Illinois, or of any other municipal corporation within the State, only that the city of Galesburg shall not, in any way or manner, be liable in case of the escape of such prisoner, or for his board while confined; and further, for any injury such prisoner may do to said prison or any other property while detained. The officer or person committing him shall be personally liable, and such person shall also be personally liable for the board of such prisoner; and the keeper shall not be obliged to receive such prisoner without the person having him in charge shall give sufficient surety for the payment of his board, and to make good all injury or damage he may do the prison or any other property, which may be done thereto in aid of his escape.

SEC. 5. It shall be the duty of the prison keeper to supply each prisoner with reasonable food and water, as the Council or magistrate committing may direct, and with the necessary bedding to keep him or her warm, for which he shall render an account to the Council from time to time, for allowance and payment. He shall not exercise toward any prisoner unncessary severity or cruelty; he shall not permit males and females to occupy the same apartment; he shall be careful and vigilant to prevent the escape of any prisoner, and to retake him when escaped; and when necessary to prevent the escape of any prisoner, or keep him in proper subjection, he may secure him with hand-cuffs, ball and chain, or other fastenings. It shall be his duty when any prisoner is committed to search him, and take from him any knives, arms or weapons of any kind, and such money and valuables as the prisoner may see proper to deliver to him, giving him a receipt therefor, all of which shall be restored to him when discharged; but he shall, in no event, be obliged to return to such prisoner any unlawful weapon. Any person guilty of a violation of any of the provisions of this ordinance, shall, upon conviction, be fined not more than one hundred dollars.

SEC. 6. It shall be unlawful for any person to aid or assist, or to furnish any means to any prisoner, for the purpose of aiding or assisting any prisoner to escape from said prison, and any person found guilty thereof shall be fined not exceeding one hundred dollars.

SEC. 7. In all cases where any person is in custody for non-payment of any fine assessed against him, and it is evident he is unable to pay the same, the Mayor may, in his discretion cause such person to be discharged from custody, upon such terms and conditions as he may think proper, to be endorsed on the amount of commitment, and if the prisoner fail to comply with such conditions, he may be re-arrested on the same warrant, or on another to be issued by the Magistrate, and committed again to prison, as in the first instance.

Sec. 8. In all cases of commitment, the prison keeper shall be entitled to a fee of twenty-five cents, for receiving and discharging the prisoner, to be taxed with the costs against the defendant, and collected as other fees are collected. And in all cases where a prisoner is committed to the city prison or calaboose for the failure to pay any fine and costs, and which are not to be worked out on the streets of the city, he shall pay to the keeper thirty-five cents per day for his board, and shall not be entitled to his discharge until the same is paid, except as provided in section 7.

Passed Dec. 7, 1857.

NO. 22

An Ordinance designating what shall be East and West Main Street, and providing for numbering the buildings.

Sec. 1. Be it ordained by the City Council of the City of Galesburg, That all of Main Street east of the public square shall be designated and known as East Main Street, and the portion west of the square as West Main Street.

Sec. 2. It shall be the duty of the Street Commissioner to provide suitable and proper numbers, and put one in a conspicuous place over or about the front door of each tenement, between the east side of the square and Prairie Street, commencing number one on the building occupied by A. D. Reed & Co. as a banking house, on lot No. 15, block No. 18, using only the odd numbers, in their numerical order, on the north side of the street, and on the south side of the said Main Street, commencing with number two on Lot No. 3, Block No. 25, using only the even numbers, in their numerical order, on the south side of said street.

For furnishing and putting up each number as aforesaid, the owner of the property shall pay said street commissioner the sum of fifty cents, for which, upon failure or refusal to pay, he shall be liable to an action in the name of the city for double the amount of said sum.

Passed Dec. 14, 1857.

NO. 23.

An Ordinance to provide for the assessment and collection of taxes, and for the non-payment thereof, in the City of Galesburg.

SEC. 1. Be it ordained by the City Council of the City of Galesburg, That to defray the general and contingent expenses of the city, an assessment list of all the real and personal property within the city of Galesburg, made taxable by the laws of the State of Illinois, for State purposes, with a valuation thereof, shall be made by the City Assessor each year, and returned to the Council on or before the first of August, unless the time for making the return thereof be extended by an order made on the records of the Council.

SEC. 2. On the return thereof, the Council shall fix a day for hearing objections thereto at the Council chamber, and the Clerk shall give one week's notice of the time of such hearing byone publication in the newspaper publishing the ordinances of the city, and any one aggrieved by the assessment of his or her property, may appear at the time specified and make objections, and the Council make such alteration and correction as to them shall seem proper, either by altering, adding to or taking from the same, or by referring the same back to the Assessor for that purpose, to be corrected by him within such time as the Council may determine.

SEC. 3. It shall be the duty of the Council at any time, and of the Treasurer at any time after the warrant for the collection of taxes shall come into his hands, to add to and supply omissions by the Assessor in making the general assessment. And the real or personal property of any one, which the Assessor has for any cause omitted, shall be by the Council or Treasurer assessed and collected at any time before settlement with the Treasurer for the current year, and by the Treasurer entered on the warrant of collection, on a page headed "Assessments made by the Council and Treasurer, omitted by the Assessor," and opposite each assessment an entry shall be made, showing whether it was made by the Council or Treasurer.

SEC. 4. It shall be the duty of the City Council, after the assessment list shall have been corrected and revised by them, to make an order confirming the same, and either by ordinance or resolution levy such sum on all the real and personal property in said list contained, by a certain rate per cent., and if for different purposes, the rate per centum for each different purpose, according to the valuation thereof, and also upon all such real and personal property in said city omitted to be assessed by the Assessor, which shall come to the knowledge of the Council or Treasurer, to be assessed and described as hereinbefore provided, as may be sufficient for the several purposes of the city, for which taxes are authorized to be levied—to be levied and collected upon all of said property equally, according to the said rate per centum and valuation thereof.

SEC. 5. It shall thereupon be the duty of the Clerk to extend and set down in said assessment list, in a column opposite the valuation of the real and personal property therein, the amount of taxes, at the rate per centum fixed by the Council as aforesaid, and if taxes are levied for different purposes, each column shall be headed with the name of the tax therein set down, and the amount thereof shall appear in the different columns.

SEC. 6. By the first day of October in each year, unless further time be given by the Council, it shall be the duty of the Clerk to issue to the Treasurer of said city a warrant for the collection of said taxes, taking his receipt therefor, and charging him with the amount. Said warrant may be affixed to said assessment list, or on one of the blank leaves thereof, and said assessment list, or the book or pages thereof, or a copy of the same, shall be made a part of said warrant, which shall be signed by the Mayor and Clerk, with the seal of the city thereunto affixed. Said warrant shall contain a command to the Treasurer to collect all the taxes on all the real estate and personal property therein contained, and also a tax of such per centum as shall be fixed by the Council for the current year, on all the real and personal property in said city omitted to be assessed by the Assessor, which shall come to the knowledge of the Treasurer, to be valued and assessed by him.

SEC. 7. It shall be the duty of the Treasurer, immediately after said warrant shall have come into his hands, to give notice thereof by handbills posted in different parts of the city, and proceed to the collection of said taxes, but he shall in no case be compelled to make personal call or demand for the same. If any person who has not paid his taxes shall have moved, or be about to move from said city at any time, not leaving property sufficient therefor, or if from any cause he shall fear such tax will be lost, it shall be the duty of the treasurer to distrain, seize and sell sufficient personal property of such person to pay the same, giving five day's notice of the sale by advertisement in three public places of the city, charging in such case in addition to such taxes, a sum equal to what constables are allowed in cases of levy and sale on execution, as compensation therefor, and returning the overplus, if any, to the owner on demand, and for that purpose, said warrant shall be sufficient authority.

SEC. 8. After the first day of January of each year, he shall return to the council a description of all the real estate on which the taxes remain unpaid, with the names of the owners thereof, and the amount due on personal property, and from whom due, which return may be made by returning to the council said warrant, noting on same in such a way as he may see proper, on what property, and from whom the same may be due.

SEC. 9. Upon said return being made, the council shall cause a description of all the premises on which the taxes remain unpaid, to be entered on the records of the council in figures, or words, or both, and the amount of taxes due thereon, and make an order, that on the first day of March thereafter, or such other time as the council may determine, all such delinquent premises shall be sold by the Treasurer in front of the Council Chamber, in said city, for the payment of such taxes and such costs.

SEC. 10. It shall be the duty of the City Clerk to make a copy of said order of Council, with a description of the premises on which the taxes remain unpaid, with the amount of taxes due thereon, certified under the corporate seal of said city, signed by the Mayor or presiding officer and Clerk, which shall be delivered to the Treasurer, and constitute the process by which the sale shall be made.

SEC. 11. It shall thereupon be the duty of the Treasurer to advertise such premises in the newspaper publishing the ordinances of the city, for sale. The publication shall be at least thirty days before said first Monday of March, or other time fixed by the Council for the sale, describing the premises by figures or otherwise, with the name of the owner, when known, and the several amounts of taxes and assessments thereon. Said notice shall contain the time and place of sale, and be published four times; provided, however, that all proceedings may be stayed for the sale of any piece of ground at any time upon payment of the taxes, costs and other expenses.

SEC. 12. It shall be the duty of the Treasurer to proceed, on the day fixed for the sale, in front of the Council Chamber in said city, between the hours of nine o'clock in the forenoon and six o'clock in the afternoon, to sell all the lands or lots on which the taxes then remain unpaid, or so much thereof as may be necessary. The sale shall be made for the smallest portion of ground to be taken from the east side of the premises, which any person will take and pay the amount of taxes, assessments, interest and costs chargeable thereon; and said sale may be continued from day to day, in the discretion of the Treasurer. The person bidding off any tract of land or lot, shall pay the collector the amount of his bid immediately, and upon failure so to do, he may offer the premises for sale immediately, or any time within five days thereafter, without further notice; and if the premises do not bring the amount of the first bid, the first bidder shall be liable by suit on the difference.

SEC. 13. Duplicate certificates of sale shall be made and subscribed by the Treasurer, one of which shall be delivered to the purchaser, and the other filed in the office of the Clerk, containing the name of the purchaser, a description of premises sold, the amount of taxes, assessments and costs for which the same was sold, and when the time of redemption will expire. And the Treasurer shall have power to complete and perfect any insufficient description of any piece of ground sold by him.

SEC. 14. It shall be the duty of the Clerk to attend all sales made by the Treasurer, and keep the record thereof; and when certificates of sale are filed with him, to keep a record of the same, which shall be open to public inspection at all reasonable times. Such record shall be ruled in separate columns, and properly headed, to indicate the contents of the columns.

SEC. 15. The owners of any premises sold, or their assigns or creditors, shall have the same time to redeem the premises sold, that is given by the State of Illinois, in force at the time of the sale, by the payment in specie of double the amount for which the same was sold, and all the taxes which may have accrued, be chargeable or have been paid on said premises subsequent to said sale, with interest. Said payment may be made to the purchaser of the premises, or other person entitled to the same, or the City Clerk.

SEC. 16. If the premises described in any certificate of sale shall not be redeemed within the period fixed by law, as aforesaid, the owner of the certificate, upon payment of all taxes and dues upon the same, and not otherwise, shall be entitled to a deed for the same at any time thereafter, upon return of said certificate to the Clerk, or proof of its loss, to the satisfaction of the Council. Such deed shall be under the corporate seal of the city, signed by the Mayor or presiding officer of the Council, and countersigned by the Clerk. But before any person shall be entitled to a deed for any premises sold for non-payment of taxes, he shall comply with section four of article nine of the Constitution of the State of Illinois, and produce to the proper officer proof thereof.

SEC. 17. If from any cause, taxes on any property, real or personal, shall not be paid for any current year, it shall be lawful for the City Treasurer, the following year, to charge the said tax to the person or property against whom or which it was assessed, and collect the same as other taxes are collected, and with like powers and remedies, to enforce the collection thereof.

SEC. 18. It shall be the duty of the City Clerk to attend all sales for city taxes, and in all cases where property, real or personal, is offered for sale, and no person will bid enough on same to pay taxes and costs, he shall bid in the same for the city; and thereupon the city shall receive, in the corporate name, a certificate of the sale thereof, and be vested with the same rights as other purchasers, and may sell or dispose of all or any of said certificates, as the Council shall see proper, or as the Mayor and City Clerk may in their discretion direct.

SEC. 19. If any tax shall not be paid by the first day of January of any year, the Treasurer shall have power to collect said taxes at any time thereafter, with interest and costs, by suit, in the corporate name of the city, or by distress and sale of personal property, and nothing contained in this ordinance shall be construed to prevent or limit the collection by suit, or distress and sale, in all cases when the Treasurer or Council shall see proper to do so.

SEC. 20. The following fees and compensation shall be allowed to the following officers and persons for services rendered, under the provisions of this ordinance:

To the City Treasurer—for returning to the Council the delinquent list—on each lot or tract of land separately listed and returned, five cents; for making out delinquent list for publication, and carefully examining and correcting proof-sheet, on each lot, five cents; for selling each lot or parcel of land, ten cents; for making out and returning each certificate of sale, ten cents.

To the City Clerk—for preparing warrant for sale for Treasurer, on each lot or tract of land separately listed and returned, five cents; for attending Treasurer's sale and making minute thereof, on each lot or parcel of land, ten cents; for recording certificate of sale, twenty-five cents.

To the Printer—For publishing notices and delinquent list, under the direction of Treasurer—on each lot or tract of land, or portion thereof separately described, five cents, to be paid by the city, and afterwards taxed and collected as other costs against the land; but the other fees herein provided for shall be charged upon the property, and the city shall not be liable for the same.

SEC. 21. On or before the last meeting of the Council in March of each year, the Treasurer shall make a full and final settlement with them, and comply with such order as they shall make in the premises. This ordinance shall take effect and be in force from and after its publication, and all provisions of all ordinances in conflict with this, are hereby repealed.

Passed, Feb. 1, 1858.

NO. 24.

An Ordinance declaring certain Roads and Highways in the City of Galesburg to be Streets, and providing for Repairing the Streets, Alleys and Bridges of the City.

SEC. 1. Roads and Highways declared to be Streets.
2. Who shall labor on Streets, Amount and Commutation thereof.
3. Labor and Money, how expended.
4. Proceedings and notice for working Streets.
5. Street Commissioner shall purchase Tools, &c.
6. Penalty for Laziness or Disorderly Conduct.
7. Repealed.
8. Settlements with Street Commissioner.

SEC. 1. Be it ordained by the City Council of the City of Galesburg, that all the lawfully established public roads and highways within the corporate limits of said City be, and they are hereby declared public streets, and where they run in the same direction as the street connecting with the same, they shall be designated and known by the name and be an extension of such street.

SEC. 2. Every male resident of said City over the age of twenty-one years, and under fifty years, shall labor two days in each year upon the streets and alleys of the City, at such time or times, and place or places, within his Ward, as the Street Commissioner shall direct, but any person may, at his option, pay in lieu thereof, one dollar for each day required, to the Street Commissioner.

SEC. 3. It shall be the duty of the City Street Commissioner to expend upon the streets, alleys and bridges of the city all the labor, and money paid in lieu of labor, as aforesaid, and such other appropriations as the City Council shall make from time to time for that purpose, when the same is most needed, or where the Council may direct, and as soon as he shall discover, or be notified of, obstructions, breaks, holes or dangerous places in the same, it shall be his duty to cause them to be removed or repaired as speedily as possible.

SEC. 4. It shall be his duty, as early after the first day of April in each year as practicable, or the condition of the streets, alleys and bridges require, to cause every resident of the city within his knowledge, and subject to labor as aforesaid, to work two days in each year on said streets, alleys or bridges, or to expend for the repair of the same the two dollars which each is permitted to pay in lieu thereof. For

14

that purpose, he shall lay off, from time to time, the respective Wards of the city into districts, according to his convenience, and determine when and where the streets and alleys therein shall be worked or repaired, and who shall do the same, and when all or a large number of persons in a particular district are required to labor as aforesaid, he shall notify them when, and the district in which the streets or alleys are required to be worked, by printed or written, or partly printed and partly written notices, posted up in three public places in the Ward, ten days before said labor is to be commenced, or published for ten days in the newspaper publishing the ordinances of the city, which notices may be in the following form, or as near as may be:

"To all male residents over 21 and under 50 years of age, in the following district, (describing it by streets or other bounds,) in the ——— ward, of the City of Galesburg—

You are hereby notified to appear on the ——— day of ———, at ———, for the purpose of laboring on the streets and alleys in said district, —— day, ——."

Or, he may require particular persons to work the same, by leaving such notice, directed to such person, at his usual place of abode or business, five days before the labor is required as aforesaid; and at the appointed time, if, from unfavorable weather, or other cause, in the opinion of the commissioner, it be best not to proceed with said work, he may adjourn the same to a future day, at which time the persons shall meet and labor as aforesaid without further notice; and if it be found unnecessary for such persons to work the number of days they were notified to do, the commissioner may discharge them and require the remainder of the two days' labor at any future time after notice as aforesaid. Upon the neglect or refusal of any person to appear and labor as aforesaid, or pay the tax in lieu thereof within ten days after notification, one dollar for each day such person was notified to work, with costs of suit, may be recovered in the name of the city from such delinquent, and the street commissioner shall be a competent witness in such suit to prove any fact within his knowledge.

Sec. 5. It shall be the duty of the commissioner to purchase, at the expense of the city, all necessary tools, scrapers, plows and other implements which may be necessary for doing any of said labor, which he shall carefully preserve; and he shall be accountable for any loss or disappearance of the same resulting from his negligence; and he is hereby furnished with full power to provide a place, at the expense of the city, for the keeping or storing thereof.

Sec. 6. If any person required to work on said streets and alleys shall be guilty of quarreling, disorderly conduct, or laziness, while engaged in or about said labor, he shall be fined any sum not exceeding five dollars.

Sec. 7. It shall be the duty of the City Assessor, when making his general assessments for the city, to make and return to the City Clerk, on or before the first day of July in each year, a list of all male residents of the city, between the ages of twenty-one and fifty, as aforesaid, a copy of which shall be furnished by said Clerk to said Street Commissioner within ten days thereafter, and it shall be the duty of said Street Commissioner, if he have not done so before, to require of all persons upon said list to work two days on the streets and alleys, or pay one dollar for each day of their refusal to do so. But in all cases where the labor, or money in lieu thereof, has been furnished before said list came into his hands, the person furnishing the same shall be credited therewith. Said Commissioner may add to such list in all cases of omission by the Assessor. If any person, not a resident of said city, or not within the ages aforesaid, shall be placed on said list, either by the Assessor or Commissioner, he shall be discharged from such liability by the City Council, upon proper proof or affidavit, at any time.

Sec. 8. It shall be the duty of the Street Commissioner, in all cases where it is practicable to do so, to take a proper voucher for all payments of money made by him; and the first of July, October and January, of each year, he shall make a return to the Council of all receipts and expenditures of money made by him, with the vouchers for his payments, and the persons from whom all moneys were received; and the last week in March he shall make final settlement with the Council.

All ordinances of the town of Galesburg in conflict with any of the provisions hereof, are hereby repealed.

Passed April 16, 1857.

NO. 25.

An Ordinance to amend the ordinance passed April 16, 1857, *providing for labor on the streets, alleys and bridges of the City.*

SEC. 1. Be it ordained by the City Council of the City of Galesburg, That it shall be the duty of the Clerk, within the month of April of each year, to make out as many lists as there are wards in the city, each showing, in alphabetical order, the male residents of the respective wards, over the age of twenty-one years and under the age of fifty, all of which may be in the same book, and may be prepared by the Clerk from the best means of information he can obtain, and he shall deliver the same to the street commissioner. It shall contain a command, under the seal of the city and hand of the Mayor and clerk, directed to the street commissioner, commanding him to require of each resident of said city, liable to work as aforesaid, the amount of labor, or money in lieu thereof, as the Council shall determine for the current year. Said book shall be ruled in columns, headed "Paid in Labor," "Paid in Money," and the commissioner shall make an entry opposite each name, showing whether paid in labor or money, or if not paid, the reason why not paid.

SEC. 2. At any time after the expiration of the time for labor or payment, under the notices of the street commissioner, and before the first Monday of July of each year, without longer time being given by the Council, said commissioner shall return said lists to the Council, showing by entry in the proper column, who has performed the labor, and who has paid, and the amount paid in money, and also how he has expended such money and labor.

SEC. 3. It shall thereupon be the duty of the clerk to ascertain the balance due on said lists, and hand the said lists to the treasurer for collection, taking his receipt therefor showing said balance, and charging him with the amount thereof.

SEC. 4. It shall be the duty of the treasurer immediately

to proceed to the collection from each person in said city liable to pay the same the amount in cash charged to him, with twenty-five cents in addition for his commission, by suit or otherwise, as he may see proper, without further demand. And said treasurer, upon final settlement, shall return said list to the Council, with the amount collected by him from same, and the names of all persons from whom collections cannot be made, and the reasons therefor.

SEC. 5. It shall be the duty of the street commissioner and treasurer, after the lists shall come into their hands, to add thereto the names of all persons coming to their knowledge, who were residents of said city on the first day of August of each year, or at any time prior thereto, omitted by the clerk, and require of them the labor or money in lieu thereof, as aforesaid. Provided, however, such persons shall not be required to perform said labor or pay said amount, without they shall receive notice as aforesaid, but same may be given them immediately after adding their names to said list, and if they do not perform the labor or pay the amount required in lieu thereof, within ten days after such notice, the same may be collected by suit with the commission as aforesaid.

SEC. 6. Section 7, of the ordinance passed April 16, 1857, entitled "An ordinance declaring certain roads and highways in the city of Galesburg, and providing for repairing the streets, alleys and bridges of the city," be, and the same is hereby repealed.

Passed March 22, 1858.

NO. 26.

An Ordinance for the publication of Ordinances, Notices, &c.

SEC. 1. One publication in newspaper of the city sufficient.

SEC. 1. Be it ordained by the City Council of the City of Galesburg, That in all cases where publication of any ordinance, regulation, by-law, notice or thing, is or may hereafter be necessary in said city, one publication thereof in a newspaper of said city shall be sufficient, except in cases otherwise required in the charter, or by the specific ordinance or regulation.

Passed March 22, 1858.

NO. 27.

An Ordinance for making improvements in the streets, and planking the sidewalks on the same, in the City of Galesburg.

SEC. 1. Petition by the owners of two-thirds the property.
2. What petition shall set forth. Order may be made.
3. Directions for making the improvement.
4. Warrant to Street Commissioner. Notice, what and how given.
5. Owner shall make the improvement. Otherwise the Street Commissioner. Return of warrant.
6. Order of Council on return of warrant.
7. Sale of premises. How made and by whom.
8. Directions for sale.
9. Clerk shall attend sale. Duties. Rights of purchasers.
10. Improvement may be without petition by unanimous vote.
11. How much of ordinances for planking sidewalk repealed.
12. Council may cause expenses to be levied on the whole property equally per front foot.

SEC. 1. Be it ordained by the City Council of the City of Galesburg, That whenever the owners of two-thirds of the real estate on any street or section of street, alley or highway in the city of Galesburg, shall wish to have the same graded, regraded, leveled, paved or planked, or any side or cross walk, drain or sewer, made, constructed, laid, re-laid, cleansed or repaired, or any street or section of street, alley or highway in said city, the Council may cause the same to be done, upon the petition of the owners of two-thirds of the real estate fronting the improvement.

SEC. 2. Said petition shall set forth the street, alley, highway or sidewalk, or portion thereof, to be improved, the character of the improvement, and number of front feet owned by each, and the council being satisfied that the petitioners are the owners of two-thirds of the premises fronting the proposed improvement, may make an order requiring the same to be made.

SEC. 3. When said improvement consists of planking any sidewalk, it shall be the duty of the council to determine and spread upon their records the width of the same, the quality, thickness, and character of the planks or timbers of which the walk shall be made, and make such further order in the premises as they may see proper.

SEC. 4. It shall be the duty of the clerk to furnish the

street commissioner with a copy of the order of the council, which shall be his warrant for causing such improvement to be made, who shall thereupon give to the owners who reside on the premises in front of which the improvement is to be made, a notice to make the same, in substance as follows, viz:

To You are hereby notified immediately after ten days from date of this notice, to make a plank sidewalk in front of your premises on street in the city of Galesburg. Said walk is to be feet wide. All the lumber or timber to be of The plank to be inches thick, laid on string-pieces by and to be feet apart, which shall be supported by bearers feet apart.

All under the direction of the street commissioner.

Galesburg, 18

Street Com'r.

Which shall be served on the resident owner personally, or left at his dwelling or boarding house, ten days before the improvement is to be made.

To all owners who do not reside on said premises he may give like notice, or by publishing the same once in the newspaper publishing the ordinances of the city, which shall be sufficient.

SEC. 5. It shall be the duty of the owners of the lots or lands respectively to proceed immediately after the expiration of ten days from said notice, to make the improvement in front of their premises, and finish the same with diligence. And upon failure to do so, it shall be the duty of the street commissioner to make the same immediately, charging ten per centum upon the cost therefor for his services; and as soon as the whole improvement is completed, he shall return to the council the said warrant, showing who has failed to comply with the same, a particular description of his or her lot of land, the amount due from each, whether resident or non-resident, and all facts relative thereto.

SEC. 6. The council may, at any time thereafter, determine whether they will bring suit against the owner of the lot of land, failing or refusing as aforesaid, for the amount of making said improvement, with the costs, expenses and interest thereon from the date of the return by the comissioner, or they may order the same to be sold for the amount of said improvement, cost, charges and interest, and of the costs and expenses attending the sale, of which a record shall be made in their proceedings.

SEC. 7. For the purpose of said sale, the clerk shall issue to the treasurer a warrant, under the seal of the city, signed by the mayor and clerk, commanding him that, after giving thirty days notice by four publications in the newspaper publishing the ordinances of the city, the first of which only need be thirty days before the sale, he proceed in front of the council chamber, to sell said premises to satisfy said assessment, with the costs and expenses as aforesaid, and the expenses of the sale. Said warrant shall describe the premises to be sold, for what purpose the sale is to be made, and the amount which is due, except the costs.

SEC. 8. It shall be the duty of the treasurer to proceed on said day to the sale of said premises. The sale shall be made for the smallest portion of ground, to be taken from the east side of the premises, for which any person take the same and pay the assessment thereon, with interest and costs, and be made between the hours of 9 o'clock in the forenoon and 6 o'clock in the afternoon of said day, and the sale may be continued from day to day until completed, and he shall give to the purchaser a certificate of such sale, and return to the clerk a copy thereof.

SEC. 9. It shall be the duty of the clerk to attend said sale, and make a minute and record thereof, as in case of sale for non-payment of taxes, and the same rights of redemption shall exist to the owner, or his heirs or assigns, the same rights to the holder of a certificate of sale or his assignee. Deeds shall be made by same persons upon expiration of same time, and with like force and effect, and like fees and charges may be made, as are provided in the ordinance for sale of property for non-payment of taxes.

SEC. 10. Nothing in this ordinance contained shall be construed to prevent the council, by unanimous vote, from causing any of the improvements herein provided for to be made without petition, but when ordered by unanimous vote of the council, without petition, the improvements shall be made in the same manner, and by the same persons, upon same order, and with like force and effect, as hereinbefore provided.

SEC. 11. The various ordinances in force for planking sidewalks are in no manner repealed or affected in this ordinance, except as to the manner of giving notice, which shall in all cases be as herein provided, and the remedies and penalties for failure to make sidewalks under any other ordinance of this city, shall be according to the provisions hereof.

SEC. 12. In all cases where the council see proper to do so, they may, by special order, provide that the expenses of any improvement contemplated by this ordinance, shall be levied upon the whole property in front of which the improvement is made, equally per front foot, instead of requiring each owner to make same in front of his own premises.

Passed March 22, 1858.

NO. 28.

An Ordinance regulating elections in the City of Galesburg.

SEC. 1. Elections, when to be held, officers to be elected, notices to be given.

2. Council shall appoint judges and clerks, vacancy, how supplied, place of holding election may be changed.
3. Officers to be sworn, election, how conducted.
4. Returns, how made, how decided when persons have equal number of votes.
5. Elections, how contested and tried.
6. Penalties for mal-conduct of officers or voters.
7. Clerk shall prepare poll books, tally papers, &c.
8. Compensation of officers.
9. Council fail to appoint place and officers, voters may do so.

SEC. 1. Be it ordained by the City Council of the City of Galesburg, That a general election shall be held in each ward of the city of Galesburg on the first Monday of April in each year, for all the officers required to be elected at such times by the city charter or ordinances of the city. The polls shall be opened at eight in the forenoon, and closed at six o'clock in the afternoon of said day. The city council shall determine and publish in a newspaper of the city, or by handbills, as they shall think proper, ten days before the election, the place in each ward where such election shall be held, and the names of the officers who are to hold the election. They shall also publish what officers are to be elected, and shall provide a poll-box for each ward.

SEC. 2. The council shall appoint one judge and two clerks for said election in each ward---who shall be legal voters of their ward. All ballots shall be handed to the judge, who shall call out the name of the voter and deposit the ballot in the box; but in all cases where any question shall

15

arise in or about said election, the same shall be determined by a majority of said three officers. If any judge or clerk appointed by the council shall fail or refuse to attend, or shall fail to be present at the place for holding the election within half an hour after the time for opening the ballots, the voters present may supply his place from their number, and said election shall proceed as though they were appointed by the council. The place of holding the election may be changed by a majority of the voters present, if the place appointed by the council cannot be used for the purpose.

SEC. 3. The judge and clerks shall be qualified, and shall conduct said election in all respects according to the provisions of the laws of this State for the election of State and county officers, so far as the same may be applicable.

The clerks of the election in each ward shall keep separate poll books, and record thereon the names of the voters in the order in which they shall vote. After closing the polls the ballots shall be counted, and if the number exceed the number of names on the poll books, the ballots shall all be returned to the box, and one of the officers shall draw therefrom enough ballots to reduce the same to the number of names on the poll book.

SEC. 4. When the votes shall have been counted, which shall be as early as practicable after closing the ballots, the clerks shall set down in ther poll books or other paper, the name of every person voted for, written at full length, the office for which such person received such vote or votes, and the number he did receive, written in words, which shall be, as nearly as circumstances will permit, in the following form:

At an election held at the house of ——, in —— ward, in the city of Galesburg, on the —— day of ——, 18—, the following named persons received the number of votes annexed to their respective names for the following described offices:

A. B. had —— votes for Mayor, C. D. had —— votes for Clerk, E. F. had —— votes for Alderman of —— ward, &c., &c.

All of which shall be sealed up in an envelope, and its contents endersed thereon, and delivered to the city clerk within two days. At the first meeting of the council thereafter the clerk shall open said returns and the council shall canvass the same and declare the result of the election. The persons having the highest number of votes shall be declared elected, and the clerk shall notify them thereof. In case two or more persons receive an equal and the highest number of votes shall be declared elected, and the clerk shall notify them thereof. In case two or more persons receive an equal and the highest number of votes for any office, the same shall be determined by casting lots, in the presence ef the Council, as follows:

The names of such candidates shall be written upon separate pieces of paper by the Clerk, and deposited in a hat or box, and the Mayor shall draw out one of said pieces of paper, and the person whose name shall be written thereon shall be the one elected, and he shall be so declared by the Council.

SEC. 5. The City Council shall have power to determine and decide in all cases where the election of any person to any city office is contested, and any person who shall desire to contest the validity of any election, or the right of any person declared duly elected to hold the office to which such candidate claims the right, shall give to the person whose election or right he intends to contest, or leave at his usual place of residence, notice thereof, in writing, stating the grounds on which he will contest the same. Such notice shall be served within five days after the holder of the office has been declared elected, and a copy of same notice shall, within same time, be left with the Clerk of the City Council, who shall lay same before the City Council at its first meeting thereafter. At such meeting the Council shall determine a time at which they will hear and examine said matter, fixing the same not more than ten days from said meeting, of which all parties shall take notice. Each party may have such witnesses subpœnæd as he may think proper, leaving their names with the Clerk for that purpose—who shall issue a subpœna, signed by the Mayor and Clerk, with the seal of the city affixed; and any person neglecting to obey the same, may be attached and imprisoned by the Council for contempt, or fined, as to them shall seem proper, and upon failure to pay such fine immediately, they shall be liable to an action for double the amount thereof, in the name of the City, before any magistrate of competent jurisdiction. The Council may thereupon, in a summary way, proceed to the trial of said matter, may examine the parties themselves, and the persons under oath, may receive affidavits and depositions, examine the records, poll books, ballots, and all other papers, certificate returns and matters, and decide according to the merits of the case—and their decision in the matter shall be final and conclusive. The Council shall have power to adjourn from time to time, and continue said trial as they may see proper.

Sec. 6. If any officer of said election shall knowingly and improperly receive or refuse a vote or ballot at any city election, he shall be fined not less than ten nor more than one hundred dollars; and if he shall improperly fail to produce any poll-box entrusted to him, he shall be fined one hundred dollars. Any person, not being entitled to the custody thereof, who shall take away, hide or conceal, any poll box, poll book, election return, certificate, or paper, or who shall advise, aid or assist therein, shall be fined not less than one hundred dollars.

If any person shall vote, or offer to vote, at any city election, knowing himself not to be a qualified voter of said city, and the ward in which he offers his vote, he shall be fined not less than ten dollars, and every person advising or influencing, or attempting to influence any person not qualified as aforesaid, to vote, or offer to vote, as aforesaid, shall be fined not less than ten dollars.

If any person shall obstruct the polls, by blocking up the way to the same, or place where the ballots may be received in any ward, and on request of any officer of the election, or person desiring to vote, shall refuse to give way, or if any person shall make any unnecessary noise, disturbance or hindrance to any other from voting, in or about said election, he shall be subject to a fine of not less than ten dollars.

Sec. 7. It shall be the duty of the Clerk of the city to make out, previous to any city election, poll books, and tally paper for each ward, and deliver the same, together with a poll box, to one of the officers of the election of each ward on demand, and after the election returns shall have been made the ballot boxes shall be returned to him, and he shall take charge of the same, and upon failure so to do, shall be fined not more than one hundred dollars.

Sec. 8. The Judge and Clerks of any election held under this ordinance, shall each receive as a compensation in full for their services at each election, $1.50.

Sec. 9. In case the City Council should fail to appoint a place in each ward for holding election, or fail to appoint a judge and clerks for the same, the qualified electors of such ward may assemble at the place therein where the election was held the previous year, on the first Monday in April, in each year, and appoint the place, judge and clerks, for holding an election for all such officers as are authorized by the City Charter or ordinances of the city, which shall be conducted in the same manner and with like force and effect as though the Council had made the appointments; and the returns thereof shall be made as herein provided; and if any officer shall fail or refuse to discharge any of the duties herein required, such failure or refusal shall not vitiate any election actually held as herein directed, and the fact and results thereof may be proven in any other way or manner which will establish the truth thereof to the satisfaction of the Council.

Passed, March 15, 1858.

NO. 29.

An ordinance in relation to Swine running at large within the City of Galesburg.

SEC. 1. Be it ordained by the City Council of the City of Galesburg, That swine of any kind shall not be permitted to run at large within the city of Galesburg; and all swine running at large in the streets, lanes, alleys, or other public places within said city, shall be, and are hereby, declared a nuisance, and when so found running at large, may be taken up and secured by any person whomsoever.

SEC. 2. When any swine shall be taken up as aforesaid, the taker up, after giving three days' notice of the sale, by posting in three public places of the city, may sell said swine for the best price they will bring, cash in hand. After paying twenty-five cents a day for keeping each hog, if the balance be not demanded by the owner, he shall pay it to the Clerk, who shall pay the same into the treasury, for the benefit of the owner, taking the receipt of the Treasurer thereof.

SEC. 3. Any person who shall knowingly permit his or her swine of any kind, to run at large within the streets, lanes, alleys, or other public places of said city, shall be deemed guilty of a nuisance, and fined not less than one dollar for each day each swine may be so permitted to run at large.

Passed, March 15, 1858.

NO. 30.

An Ordinance regulating the Fire Department.

SEC. 1. Fire Department, of whom to consist.
2. Duty of Engineer and assistants.
3. Members to be divided into companies, elect their own officers and make their own laws.
4. Duty of Marshal and police officers.
5. Penalty for interference, or injury to operators, &c.
6. Penalty for failure of duty of members.
7. Engineers may appoint assistants in cases of emergency. Penalty for disobedience to orders of fire officers.
8. Members of fire department, how compensated.
9. Who shall have charge of engines. &c. Penalty.
10. Duty of Engineers on the alarm of fire.
11. Powers of Engineers and other officers at fire.
12. Powers and dnties of Fire Wardens.
13. Same
14. Same
15. Penalty for piling combustibles.
16. Penalty for making fires in unsafe places.
17. Officers to wear badges at fires.

SEC. I. Be it ordained by the City Council of the City of Galesburg, That there shall be a Fire Department in said city, which shall consist of an Engineer, two Assistant Engineers, and a city Fire Warden, all of whom shall be appointed by the Council, and such fire engine men, hose men, hook and ladder, axe and saw men, and bucket company men as may from time to time be approved by the Council, and when so approved, and not otherwise, they shall be enrolled as members of the fire department of the city by the Clerk, in a book kept for that purpose. And the aldermen of said city shall, ex-officio, be fire wardens of their respective wards.

SEC. 2. The Chief Engineer, or, in his absence, the Assistant Engineers, in all cases of fire, shall have sole and absolute control over all the members of the fire department, the apparatus and machinery thereof, and in the absence of said Engineers, the same powers and authority shall be devolved upon the Mayor of the city, or any Alderman thereof.

SEC. 3. The members of said fire department shall be divided into companies, to consist of as many members as the city council shall from time to time direct, to attend to the fire engines, hose and hose cars, hooks and ladders, axes, saws and buckets and other fire apparatus. And such companies shall choose from among their own number such officers, and pass such by-laws and regulations for their own government as they shall think necessary.

SEC. 4. The marshal and other police officers shall repair immediately at the alarm of fire, to the place where the fire may be, and be active and vigilant for the preservation of the peace, the removal of idle or suspected persons, and the preservation of property in the vicinity thereof, and upon willful failure or refusal so to do, they, and each of them, shall be liable to a fine of not exceeding one hundred dollars, and removal from office.

SEC. 5. Any person who shall hinder or interfere with any city officer or member of the fire department in the performance of his duty, at, going to, or returning from any fire, or while engaged about any duty, or any person who shall drive any wagon, dray, or other vehicle on any hose, or shall in any manner cut, deface, destroy or injure any engine, hose or other apparatus, machinery or thing belonging to said city, or any portion of said fire company or department, shall forfeit not less than three nor more than one hundred dollars for each offence, and liable for all damages done said property thereby.

SEC. 6. Any member of said fire department who shall fail or refuse to discharge his duty, under any by-laws of the fire department or other regulation thereof, or under this or any other ordinance of the city, or who shall while on duty act in a disorderly or unbecoming manner, or who shall fail or refuse to obey the orders of any superior officer of said department, shall be subject to a fine of not exceeding ten dollars, and his name shall be stricken from the roll of the members thereof, upon proof of such offence to the city council.

SEC. 7. Any of said engineers, in cases of emergency, may appoint any number of assistants, for the time being, who shall have all the power and authority of said chief or assistant engineers, and all persons who shall repair to a fire shall be obedient to the orders of said chief or other engincers, the mayor or aldermen, marshal or policemen, in the discharge of their respective duties: and in case any person shall fail or refuse to perform such orders, he shall forfeit and pay not less than three dollars, at the suit of said city.

Sec. 8. The officers and members of said fire department shall be entitled to such compensation and exemptions as the council may from time to time determine.

Sec. 9. The engineer or such assistant as shall be named by the council, shall take charge of all engines, ladders, fire-hooks and other fire apparatus belonging to said city, and see that the same are kept in proper order and condition, and in their place of deposit, which shall be the engine house of the city, when not in actual use or undergoing repairs, and upon failure to keep the same in proper order, condition and place, he shall be liable to a fine of not exceeding fifty dollars, and to pay to said city all damages occasioned thereby. If any person shall take from said places of deposit any such apparatus, except under the direction of the engineer, or on the alarm of fire, he shall forfeit and pay, for the use of said city, the sum of five dollars for each and every offence, and five dollars for every twenty-four hours he shall neglect to return the same to its proper place of deposit, after being notified by the engineer or assistant so to do.

Sec. 10. The engineer and his assistants shall, upon notice of the breaking out of any fire in said city, repair immediately to the place thereof, vigorously exert their authority, and use their best endeavors to extinguish the same, and prevent the spreading thereof, and preserve and protect the property endangered by the same, and all persons are hereby required to pay due respect and obedience to their commands.

Sec. 11. During the continuance of any fire the said engineer and his assistants are hereby empowered to command and require the services and assistance of any person for extinguishing the same, and for removing household furniture, goods, wares and merchandise out of any building actually on fire, or in danger thereof, and to control and direct operations of persons concerned in extinguishing the fire, or removing property, as aforesaid, and to appoint proper guards to take care of all property so removed; and also, with the advice of the mayor and two aldermen, to command and require the services and assistance of any person for the pulling down or blowing up of any house or other building, and to perform any other service for the purpose of extinguishing the fire and prevent the spreading thereof, and also to suppress any tumult or disorder that might arise during the continuance thereof.

SEC. 12. The City Fire Warden shall in May, and also in November, or oftener if thought proper, inspect all stoves, fire-places, and other places in which fire may be kept in said city, and all stove pipes, chimneys, funnels, or other apparatus therewith connected, for the purpose of ascertaining whether the same are so fixed as not to endanger the building in which the same may be, or to which they may be attached, or to endanger any other building in the city; notify the occupants to make all necessary repairs, and see that the same are done within a reasonable time; and any such inspection shall be made on the request of any citizen at any time for the purpose of ascertaining the safety thereof.

SEC. 13. Whenever, in the opinion of the Fire Warden or Alderman of the ward, any stove, fire-place, or other appurtenance for the conducting of smoke or heat from any such place, may be in such a state as to render the keeping of fire therein unsafe, he is required to order the occupant of the building in which the same may be, or with which the same may be connected, to discontinue the fire therein, and to make all necessary and proper repairs to render the keeping of fire therein safe, in the opinion of the said fire warden or alderman inspecting the same, and if any person shall make a fire therein, and neglect to make such necessary repairs, after being ordered so to do as aforesaid, the occupant of any such building shall forfeit and pay for the use of said city the sum of ten dollars for every twenty-four hours the same may remain without such repairs being made,and used as aforesaid: Provided, however, That any person feeling himself aggrieved by the order or decision of the warden or alderman, as the case may be, may appeal therefrom to the city council, at the first meeting thereof, after notice as aforesaid; but in all cases the order of said fire warden or alderman to discontinue the making of fire therein, shall be complied with until the final decision of the city council on such appeal.

SEC. 14. The fire warden, or alderman of the ward, from time to time, and at least once in every six months, shall visit and examine every house and other tenement contemplated by this ordinance, and report to the mayor all breaches of any provision of this ordinance, that every offender may be subjected to any penalty herein provided for.

SEC. 15. No person shall, within the limits of said city, stack or cause to be stacked any hay, straw or other combustible material within one hundred feet of any building where fire may be kept; and every person so offending shall forfeit and pay for the use of said city, the sum of five dollars, and five dollars for every twenty-four hours the same may be suffered to remain, after notice from the fire warden or assistants in the ward to remove the same.

SEC. 16. No person shall build, make or kindle, or cause to be made or kindled, any fire in any frame building, plank or other temporary shed of lumber, without having a chimney, stove or vault, in which to build, make or kindle such fire; and every person so offending shall forfeit and pay for the use of said city, the sum of five dollars for every such offence.

SEC. 17. It shall be the duty of the various officers of said fire department to provide and wear at all fires suitable badges, to be determined by themselves, which badge, however, shall show the name of the office held by the bearer.

Passed March 8, 1858.

NO. 31.

An Ordinance in relation to Linwood Cemetery.

SEC. 1. Lands of the Cemetery.
2. Survey of the same.
3. Price of Lots. Deed, who to make.
4. Clerk to keep account of sale.
5. Potter's Field. Rights of city reserved.
6. Appointment and duties of sexton.
7. Duties, continued.
8. Graves shall not be dug in walks.
9. Depth of grave.
10. Penalty for removing bodies.
11. Sports forbidden.
12. Compensation.

SEC. 1. Be it ordained by the City Council of the city of Galesburg, That the premises conveyed to the city of Galesburg by the Linwood Cemetery Association, by deed bearing date the 15th day of December, 1857, and any additions which may be made thereto, be and the same is hereby declared to be the public burial ground of the city of Galesburg, which shall be continued and known as the Linwood Cemetery.

SEC. 2. The survey and plat of said grounds, as made and recorded by the said cemetery association, is hereby approved and confirmed, and all sales of lots made in said grounds on which the purchase money has been paid, or on which the same shall be paid within ninety days from this date, are hereby approved and confirmed.

SEC. 3. The prices of lots in said grounds shall be ten dollars, one half of which shall be paid down and the balance in six months to the said city clerk, who shall give the purchaser a certificate, stating the payment of the said five dollars, the number of the lot, and that the purchaser will be entitled to a deed for the same in six months, upon the payment of the remaining five dollars; and when said purchase money shall all be paid, the mayor and clerk shall make a deed for the lot to the proper holder of the certificate.

SEC. 4. It shall be the duty of the clerk to keep a separate account in a book kept for that purpose, of all said sales and payments, and as soon as any money is paid to him, he shall pay the same over to the city treasurer and take his receipt therefor.

SEC. 5. That so much of said cemetery numbered as blocks 11, 12, 13, 14, 15, shall be reserved for and appropriated to the burial of poor persons and strangers, who may not have other grounds provided for them, and the residue of the lots or blocks of said cemetery shall be reserved for the use and possession of such families and persons, and such only, as have heretofore or shall hereafter become the purchasers of the same, to be used by them as places of burial for the dead, and for no other use or purpose whatever, all of which shall be under the control of said city, subject to her ordinances, rules and regulations, and all owners of said lots or other persons shall comply with the same in the interment or removal of bodies, and in the care, ornamentation and use of the grounds thereof, and no deed or contract made with said city shall prevent the exercise on her part of any such power in her discretion.

SEC. 6. The city council shall appoint a sexton for said cemetery, who shall hold his office at the pleasure of the council. It shall be his duty to take the entire charge, control and superintendence of said cemetery, subject to the order of the council, and preserve and keep in proper repair the fences and enclosures of the same, so as to prevent its being entered by swine or other animals, and also, as far as practicable, prevent the destruction or defacing of any grave, grave-stone, tablets or monuments placed or erected in said cemetery. It shall also be his duty to point out to persons wishing to purchase, all lots for sale, and notify the clerk when and where any person has made a selection.

SEC. 7. It shall be the duty of the sexton to dig without delay all graves in said cemetery, on application to him by the owner of any lot, or other person having the right of interment therein; to attend every interment in person or by some competent deputy; to fill up and neatly trim the grave immediately after depositing the coffin; to fill up and trim all graves that have, or hereafter may, settle or sink in; to register the names and ages of all persons interred therein, and when non-residents, where from, if known, and the place of their interment, subject always to the inspection of the council, or any person interested, without fee; and he shall always keep the walks, avenues and alleys in good order and unobstructed, so that a free passage can be had to the lots.

SEC. 8. It shall be unlawful to dig any grave in the walks, lanes and avenues of said cemetery, and all graves and monuments heretofore made in said walks, lanes or avenues, after the lapse of twelve years from the publication of this ordinance, shall be leveled to the surface of the ground by the sexton, within which time it shall be lawful for the friends of the deceased, with the consent of the sexton, and not otherwise, to remove any body from any such grave, and it shall be unlawful for any person to dig any grave or inter any body in said cemetery without the consent of the sexton; and any person guilty of a violation of this section shall be fined not less than ten dollars for each offense.

SEC. 9. All interments shall be made at least five feet deep, and the grave dug at least six inches within the line of the lots, and all fencing, vaults or ornaments that may be erected by individuals on their lots, shall be erected so as not to obstruct any of the walks, lanes or avenues, or the access to any of them; and any person violating this section shall be fined not less than five dollars.

SEC. 10. It shall be unlawful to open or cause to be opened any grave, or to take up or remove, or cause to be taken up or removed, any body interred in said cemetery, without leave from the mayor of said city, and under the superintendence of the sexton; and the person in whose house or on whose premises any such body may be found, shall be deemed guilty of taking the same. Any person found guilty of the violation of this section shall be fined not less than one hundred dollars.

SEC. 11. It shall hereafter be unlawful for any person to play within said cemetery at any game of any sort or description whatever, or to cut, mark, write upon, or in any way or manner injure or deface any tree, grave-stone, tablet, tomb or monument on said grounds, or in any way cut, mark, injure or deface any fence in or around said cemetery, and every one so offending shall be fined not less than one dollar.

SEC. 12. The sexton shall be paid such compensation as the council may from year to year determine, and it shall be lawful for him to charge and collect of the person who shall employ him to dig a grave, the sum of three dollars, except for children under ten years of age, for which he shall charge but two dollars, in consideration of which he shall perform all the work about said grave provided in section seven of this ordinance; but nothing in this ordinance contained shall prevent any person from digging a grave for any deceased person, without charge.

Passed March 29, 1858.

NO. 32.

An Ordinance in relation to misdemeanors and other offences in the City of Galesburg.

SEC. 1. Firing in the City prohibited.
2. Digging in Streets and Public Grounds prohibited.
3. Builders may occupy half the street.
4. Obstruction to streets and sidewalks.
5. Occupant to keep sidewalks clean.
6. Cellar doors, pits, &c., shall be closed.
7. Houses, fences, &c., in the streets, nuisances.
8. Persons may abate, upon notice. Penalty.
9. Riding and driving fast prohibited.
10. Persons meeting shall "go to the right."
11. Shall not stop team in the street so as to obstruct.
12. Dog fights prohibited.
Cruelty to animals—indecent exposure of animals prohibited.
13. Posting on houses, when prohibited.
14. Dogs, &c., howling prohibited.
15. Town ordinances repealed.

SEC. I. Be it ordained by the City Council of the City of Galesburg. It shall be unlawful for any person within one mile of the crossing of Main and Cherry streets, in said city, without permission from the Mayor or Marshal, to fire or discharge any cannon, musket, rifle, fowling piece, pistol or other fire arms, or air guns, except in cases of necessity, or in the discharge of a public duty, or by military companies on parade, in the discharge of their duties or exercises, and every person found guilty of a violation of this section, shall be fined not less than one dollar for each offence.

SEC. 2. It shall be unlawful for any person in said City to dig or remove earth from any street, lane, road, avenue, alley or public ground or sidewalk, or by digging, plowing or other means, make or cause to be made, any hole, pit, ditch, trench, or other excavation in any street, road, alley, avenue, public ground or common, or on any lands whatsoever, which do not belong to the person digging or plowing, without permission of the owner, except where the Mayor or City Engineer shall give permission in cases of streets, sidewalks and other public grounds, but with such permission no person shall leave any such hole, pit, ditch, or excavation, uncovered or exposed in the night time, and every person found guilty of a violation of this section, shall be fined not exceeding ten dollars, and shall also be liable in a civil action for any injury resulting therefrom.

SEC. 3. It shall be lawful for any person, building or repairing any building in the City of Galesburg, or being about to do so, who shall not have sufficient room on his own premises for that purpose, to occupy one-half of the street, ground or alley fronting the same, or if on the public square, three rods of ground fronting the improvement, whereon to place the necessary materials for such building or improvement, which shall however be made to occupy as little space as convenient, and all of the same shall be removed as soon as not needed for the building, or at any time, upon the order of the Mayor or Street Commissioner. And any person who shall encumber such street, lane, avenue, square or public ground, otherwise than above provided, or who shall refuse or neglect to move any material or rubbish when required to do so as aforesaid, or within a reasonable time after the same is needed, shall, upon conviction, be fined not more than fifty dollars.

SEC. 4. It shall be unlawful for any person to injure or obstruct any sidewalk, pavement, gutter, curbing or street crossing in said city, or to stop any team, horses or other animals on the same, or to put any rubbish, offal, filth, obstruction or nuisance of any kind into or on said streets, sidewalks, lanes or crossings. Or to throw thereon any wood, coal, or other obstruction, or to cut or split wood thereon; and upon conviction, he shall be fined not less than one dollar for each offence, and one dollar for every twelve hours he shall suffer the same to remain. Provided, that every person shall have the privilege of unloading wood or coal outside of the sidewalk, but shall not suffer it to remain more than twenty-four hours, Sundays excepted.

Sec. 5. Every person occupying any lot or part of lot in the City of Galesburg, shall at all times keep the paved or plank sidewalks clear and in good order, and the gutters adjoining the same, free from any obstruction or incumbrance, and after fall of snow, shall cause the same to be immediately removed from the sidewalks into the carriage way of the street, and upon failure to comply with the provisions of this section shall be subject to a fine of not more than ten dollars.

Sec. 6. It shall not be lawful for any person in said city to leave open, uncovered or unguarded, any cellar door, pit, or grating of any vault, or other opening or passage into or under the ground, leading from any street, alley, sidewalk or other public place, nor shall it be lawful for any person to suffer any such place or places to remain in an insecure or exposed condition; and any person convicted under this section shall be fined not more than fifty dollars, and be liable for all damages occasioned thereby.

Sec. 7. If any person shall erect, build, place, construct, maintain or continue, after notice to move the same, as hereinafter provided, or cause or procure to be erected, built, placed, constructed, maintained, after notice as aforesaid, upon any street, lane, avenue, alley or highway, laid out within said city, any house, cellar, stable, shed, pen, fence or other structure whatever, the same shall be deemed and defined, and is hereby declared a public nuisance, and any person guilty thereof shall be fined not more than one hundred dollars, and be liable in the same manner for every twenty-four hours he shall permit or suffer such nuisance to remain upon any such public place after his conviction.

Sec. 8. In all cases when any person shall hereafter build, or continue, or fail or refuse to remove any house, cellar, stable, shed, fence or other structure, already erected or built upon any street, lane, avenue, alley or highway, laid out or declared, within said city, the same shall be and is hereby declared to be a public nuisance, and it shall be lawful for any person, after giving to the owner or person in possession of the same ten days's notice to move the said house, stable, shed, fence or other structure, to throw down, abate and remove such nuisance, and if the same shall be restored, it may be torn down and abated again without further notice, and the person restoring the same shall be subject to a fine of not exceeding one hundred dollars.

SEC. 9. Any person who shall ride or drive any horse, mare or mule, or other beasts of burden, violently, through or along any street, lane or alley in said city, or suffer the same to travel or run faster than ordinary or moderate gait, shall, upon conviction forfeit not less than one dollar.

SEC. 10. In all cases of persons meeting each other riding on horseback, or driving any wagon, carriage, dray, cart or other vehicle in said city, each person riding or driving shall turn off and go to the right, so as to enable such persons and vehicles to pass each other without danger or accident; and upon failure so to do, shall be subject to a fine of not more than ten dollars.

SEC. 11. No person shall stop any team or vehicle in any street, lane or highway of said city, in such manner as to prevent other teams or vehicles from passing, unless in case of absolute necessity, nor shall any person stop the same upon the regular crossings of streets and alleys, so as to prevent the free passage of persons traveling on foot; and every person found guilty thereof, shall be subject to a fine of not more than ten dollars.

SEC. 12. If any person shall be present at a dog fight of said city, when the animals meet accidently, or by design in persons, and shall, by gesture or words, encourage the dogs to fight, he shall be subject to a fine of not less than three dollars; and it is hereby made the duty of all police officers to suppress all dog fights, and arrest all persons encouraging the same.

It shall be unlawful for any person in said city to unnecessarily or cruelly beat,injure, whip or abuse any dumb animal.

It shall be unlawful within said city for any person to indecently exhibit any horse or jack, or let any horse or jack to mares or jennies, unless entirely out of public view; and any person violating this section shall be subject to a fine not exceeding twenty dollars.

SEC. 13. It shall be unlawful in said city for any person to stick, paste or put up upon any building in said city, against the consent of the occupant, any hand-bill, show-bill, picture or other representation, nor shall it be lawful to put up, as aforesaid, any indecent or lewd picture, or representation, or advertisement of any kind; and every person so offending shall be subject to a fine of not more than ten dollars.

SEC. 14. It shall be unlawful in said city to keep any dog, slut or hog, or other animals, shut up, tied or fastened, which shall, by barking, howling, or other noise, disturb the peace and quiet of any family, neighborhood or individual; and every person so offending shall be subject to a fine of not more than one dollar for each disturbance.

SEC. 15. Be it further ordained, That all the ordinances passed by the Town of Galesburg be and the same are hereby repealed.

Passed March 29, 1858.

NO. 33.

An Ordinance amendatory and additional to Ordinance No. 18, passed Oct. 5th, 1857.

Be it ordained by the City Council of the City of Galesburg, That execution may issue to collect any fine or penalty recovered under the charter and ordinances of said city, and costs; and the defendant, in default of payment thereof, shall be committed by virtue of said execution for the following term, viz., for one day for each dollar of judgment and costs, not exceeding six months, to be specified in said execution, which shall be, in all respects, in the form required by the charter.

Passed July 5th, 1858.

NO. 33 1-2.

An Ordinance regulating the storing of gunpowder.

SEC. 1. Be it ordained by the City Council of the City of Galesburg, That no person shall be permitted to keep or store gunpowder within any house, store or warehouse, or other place within the corporate limits of the city, under a penalty of one hundred dollars for every offence, unless the same is stored in a magazine located under the direction of the Mayor, and owned and kept by some person by him approved. *Provided*, That this section shall not be deemed applicable to retailers of gunpowder.

SEC. 2. No retailers of gunpowder shall keep or store any quantity thereof greater than twenty-five pounds weight in any storehouse, shop or place within the corporate limits of the city, except in the magazine aforesaid. *Provided*, also, That said quantities of twenty-five pounds shall be divided and kept in close tin or copper cannisters, containing not more than five pounds each; and no such retailer of gunpowder shall be permitted to sell, retail or give away the same in the city, after candle-lighting in the evening; and every person violating the provisions of this ordinance section, shall be subject to a penalty of fifty dollars.

SEC. 3. If any owner, pedlar or common carrier, shall unload or cause to be unloaded any gunpowder concealed in parcels, boxes or packages, purporting to be other than gunpowder, he shall forfeit and pay the sum of fifty dollars.

SEC. 4. It shall be the duty of the Mayor, when complaint is made to him by any city officer, or upon the affidavit of any citizen, stating that there is probable cause to suspect any person of keeping or concealing any gunpowder contrary to the provisions of this ordinance, to take with him the city marshal or any police officer, and search and examine any place within the corporate limits of the city, to ascertain the truth of any such allegation or suspicion; and if it be found, on examination of any premises as aforesaid, that gunpowder is therein concealed, the offender shall be subject to a penalty of fifty dollars, and a further penalty of one hundred dollars for every twenty-four hours that said gunpowder may remain within the corporate limits of the city after due notice has been given by the mayor or city marshal to remove the same.

Passed August 16, 1858.

NO. 34.

An Ordinance amendatory to an "Ordinance to amend the Ordinance relating to Animals running at large," passed July 17, 1859.

SEC. 1. Be it ordained by the City Council of the City of Galesburg, That it shall be the duty of the city marshal, upon complaint made to him by any citizen of this city, that any cattle, asses, mules, horses or sheep, are running at large in the city, contrary to the ordinances relating thereto, to proceed immediately to take charge of such animal or animals and secure them in a safe pen or pound.

SEC. 2. It shall be the duty of the marshal, within twelve hours after taking up of such animal or animals, to leave a description of the same in the office of the city clerk, who shall make a record thereof in his book kept for the purpose of registering estrays, and to post a notice thereof at the street entrance to his office for three days, or until the owner or owners of said animal may be found.

SEC. 3. Any person being the owner of any animal taken up by the marshal under the provisions of this ordinance, and dosiring to take possession thereof, may do so at any time by paying one dollar to the city treasurer, and the fees allowed the marshal in section 4 of this ordinance.

SEC. 4. The city marshal shall be allowed a fee of fifty cents for each and every animal taken up by him, as well as all necessary expenditures made by him for the purpose of securing and feeding said animals, which shall be paid by the owners thereof, and fifty cents to the clerk for registering and posting the same.

SEC. 5. If, after the expiration of twenty-four hours after notice given by the clerk in regard to any animal in charge of the marshal, no owner or claimant shall appear to claim and redeem the same as provided in this ordinance, then the marshal shall give notice that he will sell the said animal or animals to the highest bidder for cash in hand; said notice being made by one publication in either of the city papers printed in said city, or by being posted up in three public places in the city, and at the door of the clerk's office, for tweuty-four hours previous to the time of sale. The proceeds thereof, after paying all the expenses and fees allowed in this ordinance, shall be paid over to the city treasurer, and shall be subject to the check of the rightful owner of the animal sold, whenever said ownership is established to the satisfaction of the mayor and clerk, who shall draw a warrant on the treasurer for the amount.

SEC. 6. All ordinances conflicting with the foregoing are hereby repealed.

Passed August 16, 1858.

NO. 36.

An ordinance to prevent obstructions of railway crossings in the city.

SEC. 1. No railroad company or conductor, engineer or other employee of any railroad company managing or controlling any locomotive engine or train, shall stop or permit to stop any railroad train or car upon any railroad track, at the crossing of any traveled road or street intersecting such railroad, so as to obstruct the passage way across the same for a longer time than ten minutes at any one time, except it may be in time of making up trains or switching off, when a longer time is indispensable for the dilligent making up or breaking up of such trains; and such obstruction shall in no case be continued more than half an hour at any one time, or obstruct more than one street at the same time.

SEC. 2. Any railroad company, agent, conductor, engineer or employee of any company, who shall violate or fail to comply with the provisions in the first section of this ordinance, shall be subject to a penalty of not less than five nor more than ten dollars for each and every offence.

SEC. 3. Any person being aggrieved by the obstructions of any crossings by any railroad company or their agents, may enter complaint, in the name of the city, before any police justice having jurisdiction in such cases.

Passed November 15, 1858.

NO. 37.

An ordinance relating to the disposal of dead animals in the city.

SEC. 1. Any person or persons who shall knowingly suffer any dead animal belonging to him or to her, to remain within the city, or within one-half mile thereof, so as to be, or be likely to become putrid and nauseous or offensive to any person or persons residing within the city, shall be deemed guilty of a nuisance, and shall be subject to a penalty of not less than three and not more than five dollars.

SEC. 2. Any person or persons who may become aware of any animal dead and lying unburied within the city limits, shall make the same known to the city marshal, or other police officer, whose duty it shall be to notify the owner of such animal, if he can be found, and direct him, without delay, to remove or bury the same. And in case of refusal or neglect of such owner or owners forthwith to comply with the order of the marshal, said marshal or police officer having the matter in charge shall cause the same to be buried, or otherwise abated at the owner's expense, if he can be found. If not, the bill for such services may be presented by said officers to the city council, to be paid in mannér and amount according to their discretion.

Passed November 15, 1858.

NO. 39.

An Ordinance in addition to an ordinance passed May 11th, 1857, and entitled "An Ordinance to define and declare what shall be deemed Nuisances in the City of Galesburg, and to authorize and direct the summary abatement thereof, and for the punishment of misdemeanors in said city.

SEC. 1. It shall not be lawful for any person or persons to keep, have or maintain, or exercise any bowling alley, billiard table, faro bank, table or room, or any apparatus or machine for the purpose of playing therein, or thereupon, or therewith, at any game, for gain, hire or reward, or emolument of any kind, or in any manner whatsoever; and every person or persons who shall have in his or her possession, or under his or their control, either as occupant, agent or owner, any such bowling alley, billiard table, faro bank, table, room, apparatus or machine, constructed or used for the purpose aforesaid, and shall suffer or permit any person or persons to use the same, or play thereon for wager, bet or chance, or who shall, directly or indirectly, receive or bargain to receive any gain, hire, reward, emolument, or valuable consideration for such use or play, shall be deemed guilty of a nuisance, and on conviction thereof for each offence shall be fined in any sum not less than fifty nor more than one hundred dollars.

SEC. 2. In convictions under this ordinance, it shall be the duty of the court or magistrate rendering judgment to make it a part of his judgment that any of said instruments or machines used contrary to this ordinance shall be taken possession of by the city marshal, or other proper officer, and kept in some safe place by him, as the court shall direct.

Passed January 25, 1859.

NO. 40.

Relating to Wooden Buildings.

SEC. 1. Be it ordained by the City Council of the City of Galesburg, That it shall not be lawful for any person or persons in said city to erect, build or place wooden buildings upon any part or parts of the following described portion of the city of Galesburg, to-wit: On any of the lots on or fronting on Main street, between the west side of Kellogg street and the east line of the public square, or within one hundred and fifty feet each way from the line of said Main street, without the unanimous consent of all the property owners within the one hundred and fifty feet named, on the particular block in which they may propose so to erect any wooden building in the district named in this section; and every person who shall violate the provisions of this section, shall, on conviction, forfeit and pay not less than fifty nor more than one hundred dollars for every offence.

SEC. 2. The term "wooden building," used in the first section of this ordinance, shall be understood to embrace and mean all buildings or additions to buildings, tenements, houses, out houses, sheds, stables, and structures of every description, the outer walls of which are in whole or part constructed or built of wood, whether the roofs of the same shall rest upon the walls thereof, or upon wooden, iron, stone or brick uprights, posts or pillars, and that all sheds or other structures, the roofs of which shall be supported, directly or indirectly, by wooden posts, or other fixtures made in whole or in part of wood, be the same inclosed or not, are hereby declared to be within the meaning of the term "wooden buildings," as used in the first section of this ordinance.—*Provided*, That privies, designed and used exclusively as such, do not come within the provisions of this ordinance.

SEC. 3. Every person who may be duly convicted of the erection or placing of any wooden building within the purview and meaning of this ordinance, shall, within five days after such conviction, cause such wooden building, for the erection or placing of which he may be convicted as aforesaid, to be removed; and on failure, neglect or refusal so to do, he shall be prosecuted and fined not less than ten nor more than one hundred dollars, for each day such wooden building shall be suffered to remain after the said five days from and after such conviction as aforesaid.

SEC. 4. When any person shall be convicted as aforesaid,

and such wooden building shall not be removed within the said five days after such conviction, as provided in the third section of this ordinance, it shall be the duty of the mayor to issue to the marshal of said city a certificate, under his hand and the seal of said city, stating the fact and the time of said conviction, and designating the building for which such conviction may have been had, and such certificate shall be a sufficient warrant to the marshal of said city, and it is hereby made his duty to cause such building to be removed and demolished, and the costs and expenses thereof shall be recovered by action of debt, in the name of said city, of and from the person or persons so convicted of erecting the same as aforesaid.

SEC. 5. No wooden building within the limits prescribed in the first section of this ordinance, which may be damaged hereafter by fire or otherwise to the extent of forty per centum of the value thereof, shall be repaired or rebuilt, nor shall any such building, when the damages are less than forty per centum on its value, be so repaired as to be raised higher than the same was in value before the damages shall have been sustained, or so as to occupy a greater space than before the injury thereto.

SEC. 6. The amount or extent of damage that may be done to any building, shall be determined by three disinterested persons, residents of said city, one of whom shall be selected by the owner or agent of the building, the second by the mayor of the city, and the two thus chosen shall select a third, and the decision of the persons so appointed shall be in writing, and shall be final and conclusive, and shall be filed in the office of the city clerk; and any person who shall repair or rebuild any such building, without ascertaining the damage as provided in this section, or who shall repair or rebuild such building after the damage to the same shall be fixed as aforesaid, at more than forty per centum, shall be subject to a fine of not less than twenty-five nor more than one hundred dollars.

Passed March 15, 1869.

NO. 41.

An Ordinance (by the City Council) for the preservation of the public peace and morals.

SEC. 1. Be it ordained by the City Council of the City of Galesburg, That it shall not be lawful for any person to keep or maintain within said city a bawdy house, or house of ill-fame, or house of assignation, or any other building or place wherein indecent or lewd practices are indulged in or permitted; and every person convicted of any of the offences enumerated in this section, shall forfeit and pay not less than twenty-five nor more than one hundred dollars for every offence. Every person who is harbored or stays in such a place or house shall be presumed to be a keeper of the same, and shall be liable to prosecution and the penalty within this section contained.

Sec. 2. It shall not be lawful for any person to keep or remain at, or frequent any house of ill-fame or bawdy-house, within one mile from the outer boundaries of said city; and every person who shall keep, remain at, or frequent any such house of ill fame, or bawdy house, shall, upon conviction, forfeit and pay not less than twenty-five dollars nor more than one hundred dollars for every offence; and if any person sworn as a witness shall refuse to testify and give evidence in all cases touching his or her knowledge of any matter or thing in relation to any such house of ill-fame or bawdy-house, or shall refuse to be sworn in any such case, he or she shall be adjudged guilty of a contempt, and it shall be the duty of the magistrate to commit him or her, by warrant or commitment, to the city prison of said city, there to remain until such witness shall agree to testify as required; and in case any such witness shall agree to testify, and shall again when put upon the stand refuse to give the evidence required, he or she shall be remanded to prison upon every such refusal: *provided*, however, that no witness shall be punished for any matter or thing which he or she may disclose in any testimony given on a trial under this section.

Sec. 3. It shall not be lawful for any person knowingly to permit any premises owned or occupied by or under him, or under his control, to be used for any of the purposes named in the foregoing section, or to contribute in any way to such house; and any person so offending shall be fined not less than twenty nor more than one hundred dollars for each and every offence.

Passed May 23d, 1859.

No. 42.

An Ordinance Concerning Vagrants.

SEC. 1. Be it ordained by the City Council of the City of Galesburg, That the following named and described persons shall be, and they are hereby declared to be vagrants, and they shall be arrested and punished as such in the manner hereinafter provided, to-wit:

1st. All persons in said city able to support themselves in some honest and respectable employment, calling or business, and not having visible means to maintain themselves, and who live idly and without lawful employment or business, or who shall be found loitering or strolling about, frequenting places where liquor of any kind is sold, drank or kept, or staying at or lodging in groceries, tippling-houses, beer-houses, eating-houses, or houses of ill-fame, or market-place, or houses (of ill-fame or) of bad repute, ten pin alleys, billiard rooms, sheds, stables, or in the open air, either during the day-time or night.

2d. All persons in said city able to support themselves in some honest or respectable calling or business, and who lead an idle, immoral, or profligate course of life; and all persons in said city who shall be found trespassing upon the private premises of other persons, and not giving a good account of themselves, or who shall be found wandering abroad and from place to place in said city, begging, or placing themselves in the streets or other thoroughfares, or in public places, to beg or receive alms.

3d. All persons who are gamblers, pickpockets, or prostitutes who travel about through the city by day or night, or frequent or remain at gambling houses, houses of ill fame, or places where liquor is sold, drank or kept; or who remain on railroad cars or other places, and travel about from place to place, and who do not follow any lawful employment or business.

4th. All persons upon whom shall be found any gambling apparatus or device, or any slung-shot, colt, or knuckles of lead, brass or other metal, or any instrument, composition or thing, used for the commission of burglary, arson, or for the picking of locks or pockets, or for the playing of any fraudulent trick, plays or games, or for the manufacture of counterfeit money, or for the commission of any offence against the laws of this State, or the ordinances of said city, and who cannot give a good and satisfactory account of their possession of the same.

SEC. 2. It shall be the duty of the city marshal, or any police constable, watchman or other police officer of said city, to arrest, with or without warrant, all such persons as are described in the foregoing sections, and take them before a magistrate of said city, and a complaint shall be made against them in the same manner as is now or may hereafter be provided by ordinance in other cases for a violation of the ordinances of said city; and every person deemed guilty and convicted of vagrancy under this ordinance, shall forfeit and pay any sum not exceeding one hundred dollars, and the said magistrate before whom such vagrant may be convicted shall require the said defendant to give bond to the city of Galesburg, with two or more sufficient securities, in the penalty of not less than fifty nor more than one hundred dollars, conditional that he or she will, for the next twelve months after the date of said bond, be of good behavior, and betake himself or herself to some honest employment for support, and that he or she will not, during that time, become a vagrant within the meaning of this ordinance; and in case said defendant fail or neglect to enter into such bond within a reasonable time, to be left to the discretion of the magistrate, it shall be the duty of the magistrate to commit said defendant to the city prison of said city until such shall be given, not exceeding six months; and said defendant shall, during his imprisonment be fed on bread and water, unless, he pays for his own boarding. *Provided*, That in case the defendant shall immediately, on payment of his said fine and costs, depart from said city, and not return to the same again for the space of one year, he shall not be required to execute said bond; and in case defendant shall depart from said city without giving the said bond, and shall return to the said city again before the expiration of the said year, he shall be arrested by the city marshal, or any police constable, watchman or other police officer of said city, without warrant, and carried before the said police magistrate, and in default of said bond he shall be committed as herein required.

SEC. 3. It shall be the duty of the city marshal, or other officer arresting any person under the provisions of this ordinance, to carefully search such persons and their baggage, premises and places of abode, and if any gambling apparatus or device, slung-shot, colt, knuckles, instrument, comyosition or thing used for the commission of burglary, arson, or for the picking of locks or pockets, or for the playing of any fraudulent tricks, plays or games, or for the manufacture of counterfeit money, or for the commission of any offence against the laws of this State or the ordinances of said city, shall be found on their persons, in their baggage, or on or about their premises or places of abode, the same shall be seized and delivered over to the custody of the mayor of said city; and if, on the trial of such persons for vagrancy, they shall fail to give a good and satisfactory account of their possession of the same to the magistrate before whom they shall be tried, the same shall be declared forfeited to said city, and the magistrate shall enter up said forfeiture as a part of the judgment, and the said apparatus, articles or things herein mentioned, shall be destroyed by the city marshal, in presence of the mayor.

Passed May 23d, 1859.

NO. 43.

An ordinance regulating prosecutions, fees &c.

SEC. I. Be it ordained by the City Council of the City of Galesburg, That all officers making arrests shall attend as witnesses before the police court, and shall procure all necessary evidence in their power, and furnish a list of witnesses to the court or to the city attorney.

SEC. 2. Witnesses and jurors attending before any police magistrate or city justice, in any suit or action for any fine or penalty arising under the ordinances of the city, shall, in case judgment is obtained against the offender and collected of him, be entitled to the same fees as in like cases before justices of the peace, but no costs of any kind shall be taxed against or collected of the city.

SEC. 3. The city attorney shall not be compelled to bring or prosecute any suit, in any case, when he and the court may be satisfied that the complaint is instituted maliciously or vexatiously, and without any reasonable cause, and that the interests of the city will not be subserved thereby; and if any person charged with any offence shall, upon his trial therefor, be acquitted, and it shall appear to the court that the complaint or prosecution was instituted maliciously and without any probable cause, judgment may be rendered against the complainant or prosecutor for the costs arising in the case, and execution issued for collection of the same.

Passed Aug. 1, 1859.

NO. 44.

An ordinance to maintain peace and quiet on the Sabbath day.

SEC. I. Be it ordained by the City Council of the City of Galesburg, That it shall be unlawful for any person in said city, on the first day of the week, commonly called Sunday, to engage in any ordinary labor, trade or business, or to keep open any house of trade, shop, saloon, store, grocery or restaurant, or any place of business or amusement; and any person convicted of any of the offenses enumerated in this section, shall forfeit and pay not less than five dollars nor more than one hundred dollars for every offence. *Provided*, That this section shall not extend to the sale ot medicines by druggists, nor to sales of victuals made to travelers, nor to the conveying of passengers on Sunday.

SEC. 2. It shall be unlawful for any person or persons in said city, on the first day of the week, commonly called Sunday, to engage in the amusements or exercises of dancing, jumping, skating, running foot races, running horses, playing at ball, ten-pins, billiards, cards, marbles or other games, wrestling, boxing, pitching quoits, hunting, or any amusements or exercises of a like nature; and every person convicted of any of the offenses enumerated in this section, will forfeit and pay not less than three dollars, nor more than one hundred dollars for every offence.

SEC. 3. Whoever shall, within the limits of said city, disquiet or disturb any congregation or assembly met for religious worship, by making a noise, or by any rude, indecent, or ungentlemanly behavior, or profane discourse within their place of worship, or so near the same as to disturb the order or solemnity of the meeting, shall be deemed guilty of a misdemeanor, and upon conviction thereof shall be fined in any sum not exceeding one hundred dollars.

Passed August 15, 1859.

NO. 45.

An Ordinance to repeal Ordinance No. 38.

SEC. 1. Be it ordained by the City Council of the City of Galesburg, That ordinance number thirty-eight, (38) entitled "An ordinance to amend an ordinance number seventeen, (17) passed September 28th, 1858, entitled 'an ordinance relating to hotel runners and porters in the city of Galesburg,'" be and the same is hereby repealed; and that ordinance number thirty-five, (35) with the exception of section number five, (5) passed October 5, 1858, entitled "An ordinance to amend an ordinance number seventeen, (17) passed September 27th, 1857, entitled 'an ordinance relating to hotel and other runners and porters in the city of Galesburg,'" be substituted in its stead, and be in force from and after this day.

Passed August 29, 1859.

The following is a true copy of Ordinance No. 35, as revised and re-adopted:

SEC. 1. Be it ordained by the City Council of the City of Galesburg, That it shall be unlawful for any hotel to have more than one runner or porter on the ground of any railroad company, whose depot is within the limits of said city, to solicit passengers.

SEC. 2. Each runner or porter is required to wear a badge, bearing the name of the house which he represents, and each proprietor shall be responsible for the acts of his runner or porter.

SEC. 3. The proprietors of hotels, if engaged in soliciting passengers, shall be considered as runners, and subject to the same rules and penalties.

SEC. 4. It shall be unlawful for any person to talk in a loud and boisterous manner on the depot grounds, or to call the name of any house in a loud or boisterous manner, or otherwise unnecessarily disturb the peace, quiet and order of the city.

SEC. 5. It shall be unlawful for any runner to obstruct the passage way for passengers to and from the railroad cars upon the arrival of any train.

SEC. 6. No person shall solicit passengers in the passenger building.

SEC. 7. The penalty for the violation of any part of the above ordinance shall be a fine not less than three nor more than ten dollars.

SEC. 8. A policeman shall be stationed at the depot, whose duty it shall be to enforce this ordinance, and to arrest, with or without process, on the spot, any person found violating any of its provisions, who shall not be discharged from custody until payment of the fine and costs; and the magistrate may, in default thereof, commit him to the calaboose, or to work on the streets or other public works of the city.

Passed Aug. 29, 1859.

NO. 46.

An ordinance to repeal section number one of ordinance number twenty, entitled "An ordinance to regulate teams, fast riding, and hitching, in the City of Galesburg," passed November 23d, 1857.

SEC. 1. Be it ordained by the City Council of the City of Galesburg, That section number one of ordinance number twenty, which is in the following words—"Be it ordained by the city council of the city of Galesburg, That it shall be unlawful to leave any horse, mule, or team of any kind standing in any street or public place in said city, unless the animal or team is securely fastened or hitched, or is in the care of the owner or driver of the same,"—be and the same is hereby repealed.

Passed October 31, 1859.

NO. 47.

An ordinance to repeal section number nine of "Ordinance Number Five," passed May 11th, 1857.

SEC. 1. Be it ordained by the City Council of the City of Galesburg, That section number nine (9) of ordinance number five, (5) which is in the following words—"It shall be unlawful for any person to put any obstruction, boxes, ashes, offal or rubbish whatever, upon or into any street, sidewalk, lane, alley, public square or gutters of said city; and upon conviction thereof, any person so offending shall be fined not exceeding ten dollars, and it shall be the duty of the occupant of the premises fronting on any sidewalk or gutter to keep the same clear of snow and ice, manure or other offal, or rubbish, and upon failure to do so, the street commissioner shall cause the same to be done at the expense of such occupant, for which he shall be liable, upon suit in the name of the city; *provided*, however, that this section shall not apply to cases of removal, receiving or sending away goods, where not more than one-third of the sidewalk is occupied, nor shall it apply to the use or occupation of one-third of the sidewalk, on the side next the building, for the purpose of showing and exhibiting goods, wares or merchandise,"—be and the same is hereby repealed.

Passed February 27, 1860.

NO. 48.

An ordinance in relation to certain sidewalks.

SEC. 1. Be it ordained by the City Council of the City of Galesburg, That the order passed for a sidewalk on the west side of Chambers street, from Main to North street, be and the same is hereby repealed; and that a sidewalk be built on the east side of Chambers street from Main to North street, four feet in width, under the direction of the street commissioner, whose duty it shall be to notify the parties in interest according to law.

NO. 49.

Resolution regulating fees of city officers in section number four (4) *in ordinance number thirty-four*, [34] *and in relation to cattle running at large.*

SEC. 1. On motion it was ordered that the fees allowed city officers in section number four (4) in ordinance number thirty-four (34) relating to the taking up of cattle running in the streets at night be reduced one half, and that the time for advertising and selling shall be six days instead of three, as now.

Passed August 29, 1859.

NO. 50.

An ordinance to amend ordinance number Nine.

SEC. 1. Be it ordained by the City Council of the City of Galesburg, That ordinance number 9, passed June 22d, 1857, be and the same is hereby amended, in so far as it relates to the keepers of meat markets, so that licenses to butchers having less than one year to run, may be charged for at such rate as the city clerk may in his discretion direct.

Passed January 21, 1861.

NO 51.

An ordinance to amend "an ordinance (number one) to define and declare what shall be deemed a nuisance in the city of Galesburg, and passed May 11*th,* 1857.

SEC. 1. Be it ordained by the City Council of the City of Galesburg, That section number eight of ordinance number one, passed May 11th, 1857, be and the same is hereby amended so as to read as follows: "Every person receiving a license from said city, either as a druggist, or any other person who shall be licensed to keep any vinous or alcoholic liquors for sacramental, mechanical, or medicinal purposes, shall not be allowed to sell any such vinous or alcoholic liquors for medicinal purposes, without such person having, and presenting for inspection, a prescription from a practicing physician, stating that he believes that such person needs the kind of liquor prescribed for him as a medicine. And further, the person so licensed as aforesaid shall keep a book of account of all liquors sold by him, the date of such sale, the kind of liquor sold, to whom sold, the amount of each sale and the amount received for the same, which book shall be open at all times to the inspection of the mayor, aldermen, or city attorney of said city; and for a failure to comply with the requirements aforesaid, he shall be liable to all fines and penalties imposed by ordinance number one for selling liquor without leave.

SEC. 2. Be it further ordained, That any person licensed as aforesaid, who shall sell vinous or alcoholic liquors for mechanical or sacramental purposes, shall be responsible if the liquor sold by them shall be used for the purpose of drinking the same as a beverage, and if it be proven that the liquor is sold as aforesaid and used for the purpose of drinking as a beverage, the person so selling as aforesaid shall be liable to all the fines and penalties imposed by Ordinance Number One aforesaid, for selling liquor without a license.

Passed February 4, 1861.

NO. 52.

An ordinance to amend "ordinance No. 23, passed Feb. 1, 1858," entitled "an ordinance," &c.

SEC. 1. Be it ordained by the City Council of the City of Galesburg, That section number eighteen (18) of ordinance number twenty-three, (23) passed February 1st, 1858, entitled "an ordinance to provide for the assessment and collection of taxes, and for the non-payment thereof, in the city of Galesburg," be and the same is hereby amended by adding thereto the following words—"or as the mayor and city clerk may, in their discretion direct."

Passed February 18, 1861.

NO. 53.

An ordinance to amend section number one of ordinance number thirty-nine, passed Jan. 25th, 1857.

SEC. 1. Be it ordained by the City Council of the City of Galesburg, That section number one [1] of ordinance number thirty-nine [39] passed January 25th, 1859, be and the same is hereby amended, by adding to said section the following words, to-wit—"without such person or persons have a license from the city council permitting such games, and the conditions on which they may be played."

Passed January 6, 1862.

NO. 54.

An ordinance amending section five of Ordinance No. 32, relative to sidewalks in the city of Galesburg.

Be it ordained by the City Council of the City of Galesburg, That the owner of any lot or part of a lot in the city of Galesburg, whether said lot or part of lot is occupied by himself or herself, or tenant, or whether the same is vacant and unoccupied, shall at all timeskeep the sidewalk adjoining the same free from obstruction and in good order, and shall within ten hours after a fall of snow remove or cause the same to be removed from the sidewalk; and upon failure so to do, in compliance with this ordinance, it shall be the duty of the street commissioner to clear the walk or walks so obstructed by snow, and he shall, within ten days, render an account of such service, with the expense thereof, to the city clerk, with a particular description of the lot or lots in front of which the walk or walks have been so cleaned by him, or his order, which expense shall be taxed against said lot or lots, and added to and collected with other city taxes, on the same premises.

NO. 54 1-2.

An ordinance concerning saloons and restaurants.

Be it ordained by the City Council of the City of Galesburg, That the license for keeping an eating saloon or restaurant in this city shall be one hundred dollars per year, from and after this date, and that the part of ordinance number nine, fixing the license for the above pursuits at ten dollars be and the same is hereby repealed.

Passed May 6, 1852.

NO. 55.

An Ordinance regulating the weighing, measurement and sale of wood, hay and coal in the City of Galesburg.

SEC. 1. Be it ordained by the City Council of the City of Galesburg, That there shall be appointed by the city council, a city inspector of hay, coal and wood, who shall attend at the public scales at all reasonable hours during the day, or be in close proximity thereto, for the purpose of weighing or measuring each load or parcel that may be presented to be weighed or measured. He shall keep an appropriate book, in which he shall enter the kind, weight or measurement of each load or parcel weighed or measured, and for whom, and the date when weighed or measured, and shall give a certificate thereof to the person applying for the weighing or measurement of such load or parcel, which certificate shall be paid for at the time of weighing, and delivered over by the owner of the load or parcel to the purchaser thereof, at the time of the delivery of the same.

SEC. 2. No person shall be appointed, or be competent as city inspector, who shall, directly or indirectly, follow the business of buying, selling or delivering wood, hay or coal.

SEC. 3. The city clerk shall procure a book and printed blank certificates for the use of the inspector, and shall number the same and deliver them to him, taking his receipt for the number thereof, and charging him at the rate of ten cents for each blank certificate, and crediting him from time to time with the treasurers receipts filed by him, and other proper credits.

SEC. 4. Any city inspector who shall knowingly give any false or fraudulent certificates of the weight or measurement of any load or parcel weighed or measured by him, shall be subject to a penalty of not less than ten dollars, and may be removed from office.

SEC. 5. Any person who shall alter any certificate of the inspector, or shall use, or attempt to use, the same for any other load or parcel than the one for which it was delivered, or shall, after the weighing or measuring and before the sale or delivery of any load or parcel, diminish the quantity thereof, or shall practice, or attempt to practice, any other fraud or deceit in the weighing, measuring, sale or delivery of any load or parcel, shall be subject to a penalty of not less than ten dollars in each case; and the inspector shall use dilligence in detecting fraud or deceit, and prosecute the person or persons guilty of the same.

SEC. 6. That it shall not be lawful within the corporate limits of said city for any person or persons to buy, sell, or dispose of any load or loads of hay, stone-coal or wood, without having the former weighed on the city scales, and the latter measured by the city inspector, and obtaining from him a certificate of the quantity of the same,

SEC. 7. The weight of a ton of hay shall be twenty hundred pounds (2000 lbs.) net, and the weight of a bushel of stone-coal shall be eighty pounds, (80 lbs) and one hundred and twenty-eight (128) cubic feet of compactly laid wood shall constitute a cord.

SEC. 8. The price of weighing a load of hay or coal shall be ten cents, (10 cts.) including the weighing of the empty wagon, and the same fee shall be paid for measuring each and every load of wood, which shall be paid by the party disposing of the same, to the inspector, before he shall give the certificate required by the sixth section of this ordinance.

SEC. 9. It shall be the duty of the inspector to make out and return, at each regular monthly meeting of the board of aldermen, an aggregate amount of the receipts of the city scales and for the measurement or inspection of wood, and he shall also exhibit to the Board the receipt of the city treasurer for whatever sum may have been due the city, after deducting one-half of the net proceeds as a compensation; and if the inspector neglects or refuses to comply with the provisions of this section, he may be proceeded against as in other cases of a violation of city ordinances, and removal from office, at the discretion of the city council.

SEC. 10. It shall be the duty of the inspector to weigh all wagons and sleds used in hauling hay or coal, and he shall mark the weight of the wagon on the bed and hind axle-tree, and shall mark the sleds on the bed and fore part of runners, and he shall, from time to time, if any change has been made in any wagon or sled, after being once weighed and marked as aforesaid, and if the said inspector shall at any time suspect any change has been made, re-weigh and remark such wagon or sled.

SEC. 11. If any person or persons shall buy, sell, dispose of or purchase any load or loads of hay or stone-coal, without first having the same weighed upon the city scales, or wood without having the same measured or inspected, and procuring a certificate as aforesaid, he or they so offending shall, for each and every offence, or for each and every load so sold, bought or disposed of, or purchased, forfeit and pay for the use of the city the sum of five dollars, ($500) to be collected as other fines are collected for violations of city ordinances. *Provided*, That the provisions of this section shall not apply to any railroad manufacturing establishments or public institutions.

SEC. 12. The inspector may permit any person or persons to weigh any wagon load other than hay or coal, and shall charge such person for weighing such load the sum of ten cents, (10 cts.) and may weigh any other articles or things for any person or persons, and shall charge him or them for weighing the same the sum of ten cents.

SEC. 13. It is hereby made the duty of the city inspector and the city marshal to exercise due dilligence in seeing that all hay and coal brought within the limits of the city shall be weighed upon the city scales, and all wood inspected and measured, and when the inspector has reason to believe or suspect that any hay or coal has been sold, purchased or disposed of, which has not been so weighed, or wood so measured or inspected, he shall enter complaint before the mayor, who shall proceed against the person offending as in other cases for violation of city ordinances.

SEC. 14. It shall not be lawful for any person in said city having wood, coal or hay in market, for sale by the wagon or cart load, or loaded in or upon any other vehicle, to stop or wait with the same for a purchaser, on any street, lane, avenue, alley or public ground, except in the following places, and in the manner specified, to-wit:

Wood teams shall be permitted to stand on the north-east quarter of the public square; coal teams upon the north-west quarter of the same, and hay teams on the south-west quarter of the same; and all of said teams shall stand lengthwise along the places appropriated to each, close behind each other, leaving sufficient room for persons on foot to pass between them; and any person or persons violating any section of this ordinance not otherwise provided for, shall forfeit the sum of five dollars, to be collected as other fines are collected for violation of city ordinances.

Passed Dec. 3, 1863.

NO. 56.

An ordinance to amend ordinance No. 55.

Sec. 1. Be it ordained by the City Council of the City of Galesburg, That nothing in ordinance No. 55, passed Dec. 3d, 1862, shall apply to the weighing of hay when the same is intended to be pressed at any hay press within the limits of the city.

Sec. 2. That in cases where individuals contract for two or more cords of wood, or three or more tons of coal, the provisions of ordinance No. 55 shall work no restraint upon said parties so contracting, unless the purchaser may desire the same measured or weighed by the city inspector, in which case it shall be done at the expense of the seller, and at the cost charged in said ordinance in other cases; *provided*, however, that all parcels of stone-coal shall be sold by weight, and the certificate of the weight, either from the bank where the coal is taken, or from the city inspector, given to the purchaser.

Sec. 3. That from and after the passage of these amendments to ordinance No. 55, it shall not be lawful for any person or persons to open and keep a wood or coal yard without having procured a license from the city council for such purpose—the fee for the same to be ten dollars per annum.

Sec. 4. That all dealers in wood and coal within the city limits, regularly licensed by the city council, shall not come under the provisions of said ordinance No. 55; but they shall not be compelled to give certificates of the measure or contents of every load sold by them, and in case the same shall represent a greater quantity than the load may contain the seller shall be subject to a fine of five dollars.

Sec. 5. Any person violating any portion or section of this ordinance shall be subject to a fine of five dollars, to be collected as in other cases of violations of ordinances.

Passed Dec. 27, 1862.

No. 57.

An ordinance to amend section number eleven of ordinance number fifty-five.

Sec. 1. Be it ordained by the City Council of the City of Galesburg, That section number eleven of ordinance number fifty-five, passed December 3d, 1862, be and the same is hereby amended by adding thereto the following words, viz: "buying for their own consumption."

NO. 58.

An ordinance to repeal section number four of ordinance number fifty-six.

SEC. 1. Be it ordained by the City Council of the City of Galesburg, That section number four of ordinance number fifty-six, passed December 27, 1862, be and the same is hereby repealed.

NO. 59.

An Ordinance for the removal of Nuisances caused by dead animals lying in the city unburied.

SEC. 1. Be it ordained by the City Council of the City of Galesburg, That it shall not be lawful for any person to put, or cause to be put, or having put, to suffer to remain at any place within the limits of the city of Galesburg, any dead horse, cow, hog, dog, sheep or cat, or remains of any dead animals whatever; and any person so offending shall on conviction thereof forfeit and pay a fine not exceeding fifty dollars, nor less than one dollar, and all costs, for each offence.

SEC. 2. If any dead shall be found within the limits of the city, it shall be the duty of the person owning such animal at the time of its death, to cause the same to be buried without delay, at least one foot and a half below the surface, and so that no stench will arise from it thereafter; and if any owner or owners of any dead animal, on being informed thereof by the city marshal or any other person, shall, after reasonable notice, refuse or neglect to bury the same, it may be removed by the city marshal, or any other person, and buried at the owner's expense, or at the expense of any person known to have placed such dead animal within the limits of the city, and the same may be collected by action of debt before any magistrate of the city. *Provided*, That the payment of such expense shall not in anywise exonerate or absolve any person or persons from the fine or penalty imposed by this section, and any person or persons who shall neglect or refuse to comply with the provisions of this section, shall, on conviction thereof, forfeit and pay a fine not exceeding ten dollars, nor less than one dollar, and costs, for each offense.

SEC. 3. When any dead animal shall be found or left within the limits of the city unburied, and the owner cannot be immediately found, it shall be the duty of the city marshal, on his own knowledge, or on complaint of any citizen, to cause such dead animal to be buried at the expense of the city, and then to use all dilligence in finding the offender, and to enforce this ordinance and its provisions, as well as against all offenders wherever found.

Passed September 11, 1863.

NO. 60.

An Ordinance to amend ordinances Nos. 55 *and* 56.

SEC. 1. Be it ordained by the City Council of the City of Galesburg, That it may be lawful for any person to sell coal in this city on the certificate of its weight from any regular weigher with which the purchaser may be satisfied, and for which certificate, when issued by the city inspector, the seller shall pay five cents per load, and that any provision in any ordinance now in operation in this city to the contrary be and the same is hereby repealed.

SEC. 2. That section number two, in ordinance number fifty-six, passed December 11, 1862, be and the same is hereby repealed.

SEC. 3. That wood sold in quantities of more than one cord may be delivered to the purchaser previous to inspection and measurement; but the seller shall not be entitled to his pay for any such wood delivered, until the city inspector shall have inspected and measured the same in bulk, and for which he shall give a certificate, and shall receive from the seller ten cents per cord for all lots under three cords, and for all lots over that amount five cents per cord.

Passed Oct. 10, 1863.

NO. 61.

An Ordinance to appoint and define the duties of a Sealer of weights and measures in the city of Galesburg.

§ 1. That hereafter there shall be a regulation of weights and measures within this city, and the standard adopted by the State of Illinois shall be the test by which they shall be compared and determined.

§ 2. The common council, at the expense of the city, shall procure correct and approved standards, with their necessary sub-divisions, together with the proper beams and scales, for the purpose of testing and proving the weights and measures of said standard used in the city.

§ 3. It shall be the duty of the inspector and sealer of weights and measures, who shall be appointed by the council, to at least once in every year examine and test the accuracy of all weights, measures, scales, or other instruments or things used by any person for weighing or measuring any article for sale in the said city of Galesburg; to stamp with a suitable seal all weights, measures and scales so used which he shall find correct, and deliver to the owner thereof a certificate of their accuracy; to condemn all weights, measures and scales which he may find incorrect upon such inspection, and to cause the owner thereof to have them corrected and made to conform to said standard in the manner hereinafter provided. Any person refusing to exhibit any weights, measures or scales, or instruments for weighing or measuring, to said sealer for the purpose of examination and inspection, as aforesaid, or obstructing him in the performance of his duty, shall forfeit a penalty of not less than five dollars nor more than thirty-five dollars for each offense.

§ 4. It shall be the duty of said inspector and sealer of weights and measures to examine, put in order, and seal all weights and measures, beams and scales, at the several places where the same are used; but if the inspector shall find that they are not conformable to the standard of the State, they shall be sent by the owner thereof to such place as the sealer may direct, or the owner may choose, for the purpose of being repaired and adjusted, and the same shall be sealed within a reasonable time thereafter. Any person offending against the provisions of this section shall, on conviction thereof, be fined in any sum not less than three dollars, nor more than twenty-five dollars.

§ 5. The inspector and sealer of weights and measures shall be allowed to receive the following fees of office for services rendered by him under this ordinance, viz: For inspecting and sealing platform scales of five thousand pounds and upwards, including weights, sixty cents: of less denomination, including weights, thirty cents each; for inspecting and sealing large beams weighing one thousand pounds and upwards, including weights, twenty-five cents; of smaller denominations, including weights, fifteen cents each; for comparing and sealing any measure, bushel ten cents, half bushel five cents, for less denominations, each three cents;

for comparing and sealing wine and beer measures, each two cents; for comparing, inspecting and sealing cloth and board measures, five cents each. Fees to be paid by the owners.

SEC. 6. The inspector of weights and measures shall be entitled to charge and receive the fees as specified in this ordinance, and he shall in every case, where he may employ labor and material in making the same accurate, be entitled to a just compensation therefor.

SEC. 6. It shall not be lawful for the said inspector to make the aforesaid charges for inspecting and testing weights, measures and scales as aforesaid, oftener than once in each year, unless the same shall be found not conformable to the standard of the State.

SEC. 8. No person shall make use of any weight, scale, measure or other instrument for weighing or measuring any article for sale in the city, until the same has been duly examined and sealed by the sealer of weights and measures, under a penalty of not less than five dollars, nor more than twenty-five dollars for each offence, recoverable before any court having jurisdiction in this city. All persons using weights or measures, scales or other instruments for measuring any article for sale in this city which have been sealed, shall, upon application of the sealer of weights and measures, allow the same to be examined, tested and sealed, as herein provided, under a penalty of not less than five dollars, nor more than thirty dollars, for failing so to do; and any person or persons altering any weights, or measures, or scales, causing the same to measure or weigh incorrectly, unless to repair, shall, on conviction thereof be fined in any sum not less than ten dollars, nor more than one hundred dollars.

SEC. 9. It shall be the duty of said sealer to make a register of all weights, measures, scales, beams and steelyards, or other instruments inspected by him, in which he shall state the name of the owner of the same, the date of the examination, and whether they are conformable to the standard of the State; and in case he finds any that are not conformable to the standard of the State, he shall immediately report the fact to the mayor, and once in each year he shall deliver a copy of his register to the city clerk, who shall keep the same open to the inspection of all persons.

SEC. 10. *Provided*, nevertheless, that the foregoing section shall be of no effect until the said standard shall be provided, and a sealer of weights and measures duly appointed and sworn into office.

Passed Nov. 2, 1863.

No. 62.

Amendment to Sec. 1, Ordinance 13.

Be it ordained by the City Council of the City of Galesburg, That every owner of a dog or slut in this city, shall pay for every dog or slut that may be suffered to run at large in this city, the sum of one and one half dollars ($1,50) as an annual tax, to be paid to the city clerk for the benefit of the city, on every dog, and seven dollars ($7) on every slut, instead of the amount as named in Section 1, of Ordinance No. 13, passed June 9, 1857, which said section, so far as relates to the amount of tax per annum on dogs and sluts, is hereby repealed, and that the clerk's fees for registering each one shall be fifty cents.

Passed April 12, 1864.

NO. 63.

An ordinance to regulate city attorney's fees.

Be it ordained by the City Council of the City of Galesburg, That hereafter in all suits brought in justice's court in behalf of said city, against any person for a violation of any of the ordinances of said city, and the said person shall be convicted, the court before whom the same is tried shall tax up the sum of one dollar as city attorney's fees, which shall be collected as the other costs in the suit are collected.

Passed May 2, 1864.

NO. 64.

An Ordinance to amend Ordinance Number Fifteen.

SEC. 1. Be it ordained by the City Council of the City of Galesburg, that it shall be unlawful for Horses, Cattle, Mules, Asses or Sheep, to run at large in the City of Galesburg, and the owner, or possessor of any such animal, permitting them to run at large in said City, shall be subject to a fine, in the name of the City, of not less than one or more than ten Dollars, for each and every animal so running at large. Provided, that the above section shall not extend to Milch Cows, the owner or possessor not having but two.—But such cows shall not be permitted to run at large within said city, between one hour after sunset and sunrise. And the owner or possessor permitting it shall be subject to a fine of not less than one dollar, nor more than ten dollars, for every cow so running at large, to be recovered in the name of the city of Galesburg. And all ordinances of said city in conflict with this ordinance are hereby repealed.

SEC. 2. Be it ordained by the City Council of the City of Galesburg, that Section number Five, of ordinance number fifteen, passed July 17th, 1857, be amended as follows: That the taker up of animal or animals shall notify the city Marshal, of the city of Galesburg, who shall cause the amount thereof to be assessed as provided in said section five, and in case the Marshal is absent from the city, or is unable to perform the said duties, any other city officer may be notified as aforesaid, and he shall perform the Marshal's duty in that respect. And the persons so acting as appraisors, or in assessing damages as provided in said section five, shall be paid a fee of fifty cents, each to be collected as other costs are collected under said ordinance number fifteen.

Passed July 5th, 1864.

Attest, W. A. WOOD, City Clerk.

JOHN A. MARSHALL, Mayor.

ARTICLE IX.

ARTICLE X.

ARTICLE XI.

ARTICLE XII.

ORDINANCES.

I.

II.

III.

IV.

V.

VI.

VII.

VIII.

IX.

X.

XI.

INDEX.

www.ingramcontent.com/pod-product-compliance
Lightning Source LLC
LaVergne TN
LVHW011238110826
845150LV00006B/1675